High Probability Trading Strategies

2022

Powerful Day Trading and Scalping Strategies for Making Money In Crypto, Forex and Stocks!

Table of Contents

Introduction

Day trading can be very profitable but it can also be very risky, especially if you don't have a good strategy in place. We've put together this guide to show you the best day trading strategies for making money in the markets. These are strategies that we've used ourselves, and that have been proven to work.

Making a profit in the market is never a sure thing, but there are certain strategies that can give you a better chance of success than others. If you want to make money day trading, you need to have a good edge in the market and use a strategy that has a high probability of winning.

Our strategies are designed for traders who want to take advantage of short-term price movements in the market. We use a combination of technical indicators and price action to identify high probability trade setups for making money in the markets no matter what the market conditions are.

One of the great things about day trading is that you can take advantage of market volatility to make money. This means even in down markets you can still make money. The key is to trade high probability setups that have a good risk/reward ratio.

In this book, we will show you how to find high probability trades and how to manage your risk so that you can make money in any market condition. Our strategies are based on sound trading principles and have been tested in the markets over many years.

We will first show you the basics of finding high probability setups, then we will show you how to enter and exit trades for maximum profits.

Chapter 1: Getting Started

Before you jump in and start trading, it's important to understand the basics of how day trading works. In this chapter, we'll give you an overview of the essentials you need to know before starting out.

Day Trading and Scalping – What's The Difference?

The trading strategies in this book are for day trading and scalping, so let's take a minute to define what day trading and scalping are.

- Day trading is the buying and selling of securities within the same day. Traders who engage in this type of trading are typically looking to take advantage of short-term price movements throughout the day.

- Scalping, on the other hand, is a more aggressive approach to trading. In scalping, traders aim to make small profits by taking many positions throughout the day. They often exit their trades very quickly, sometimes in just a few minutes.

Both day trading and scalping can be profitable strategies, but they require a solid trading plan, along with good risk management techniques. Now that we have a basic understanding of what day trading and scalping are, let's take a look at how to find high-probability setups.

The Different Types of Trading Strategies and How They Work

Now let's take a look at the different types of trading strategies you can use, and what kind of market conditions to use them in:

- Mean reversion trading

- Momentum trading

- Trend trading

Mean Reversion Trading:

Mean reversion is a trading strategy that tries to take advantage of when price has moved too quickly in one direction and is likely to revert back to its mean (average price). Mean reversion strategies typically use overbought/oversold conditions on momentum indicators to identify when price is likely to revert back to its mean.

To find the mean, you can simply use a moving average like a 20 SMA or 50 SMA. Price always likes to stay close to these moving averages, and if you see price moving far away from the mean you know it is likely to pull back soon.

Market conditions: The best time to use this strategy is when the market is choppy and there is no clear trend.

One of the best mean reversion indicators is the Bollinger bands, this indicator works by plotting a moving average and two standard deviations above and below it. When price is touching the upper or lower band, this indicates it is likely to revert back to its mean.

A simple mean reversion trading strategy using the Bollinger bands would be to buy when it touches the bottom band and sell when it touches the top as you can see in the example below.

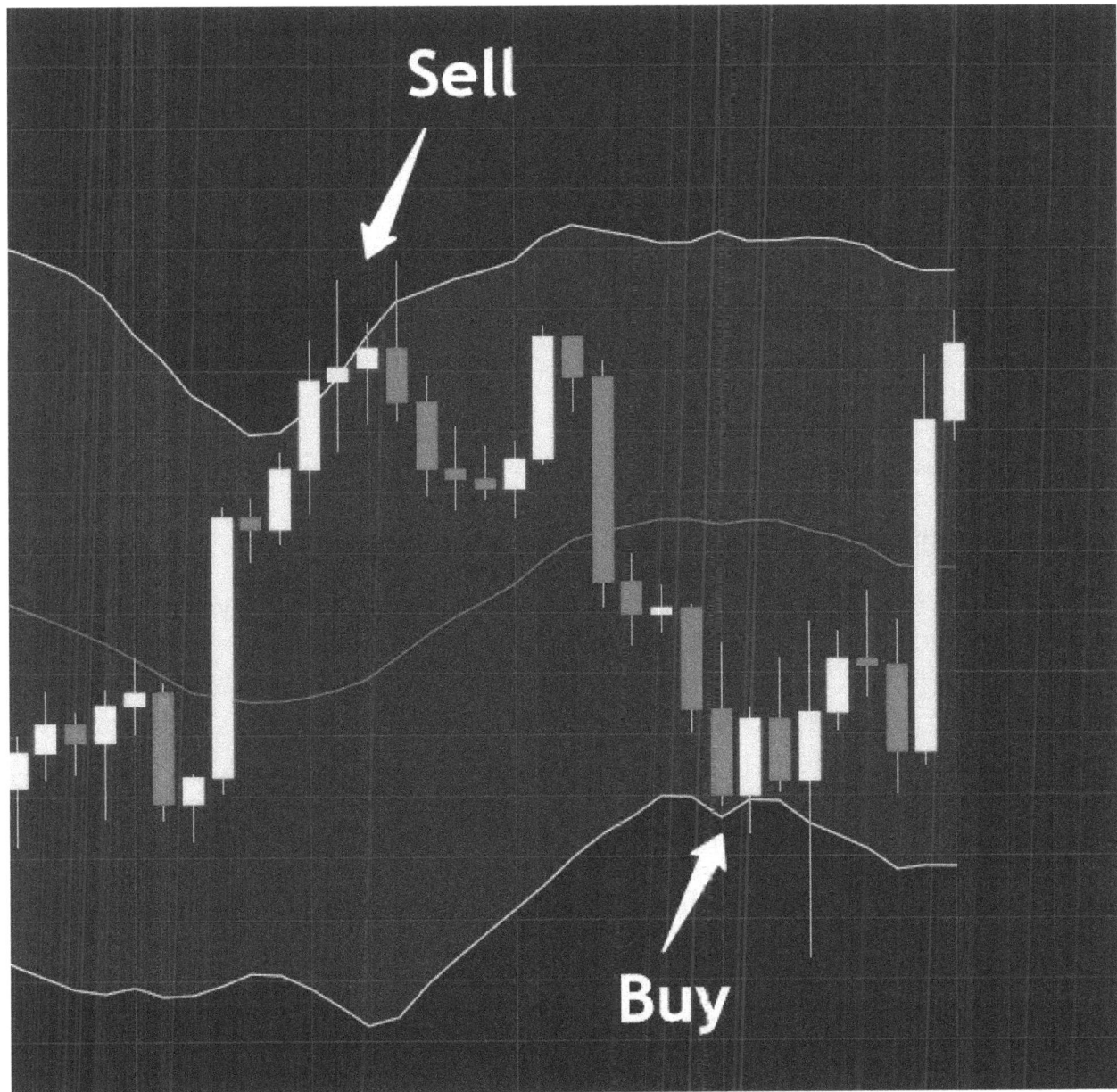

Example of a mean reversion trading strategy using the Bollinger bands

Momentum Trading:

Momentum trading uses technical indicators to help spot when a security is starting to gain momentum in either a positive or negative direction. At the very heart of momentum trading is the idea that price momentum precedes price action. In other words, the momentum of a security's price will change direction before the price itself changes direction.

This is extremely important because it means that we can get into a trade ahead of the move, rather than trying to pick tops and bottoms. When trading momentum the key thing to remember about momentum trading is that we are looking for a change in momentum, not just momentum itself. A stock can have strong positive momentum and be ripe for a long trade, but if the momentum starts to wane then it's time to get out. You want to spot these changes in momentum early so that we can take advantage of them.

We can identify changes in momentum using momentum indicators like the RSI or MACD. These indicators will typically turn down before price does, so if we see our momentum oscillators moving down while price is moving up, this is a signal that a reversal is imminent.

When used correctly, momentum trading can be an extremely effective way to make money in the markets. By getting in ahead of the move, we can often capture a large part of the move and ride it all the way to the top. Of course, like with any strategy, there are risks involved and it is important to understand these before putting any real money on the line. But if you're willing to take on a bit of risk, then momentum trading could be a great way for you to make some serious profits.

Let's take a look at an example of a how a momentum trading strategy would look using the RSI indicator. In this example we will buy when the RSI crosses above 50, and sell when it crosses below. When the RSI crosses above or below 50, this is a signal that momentum is changing in the market.

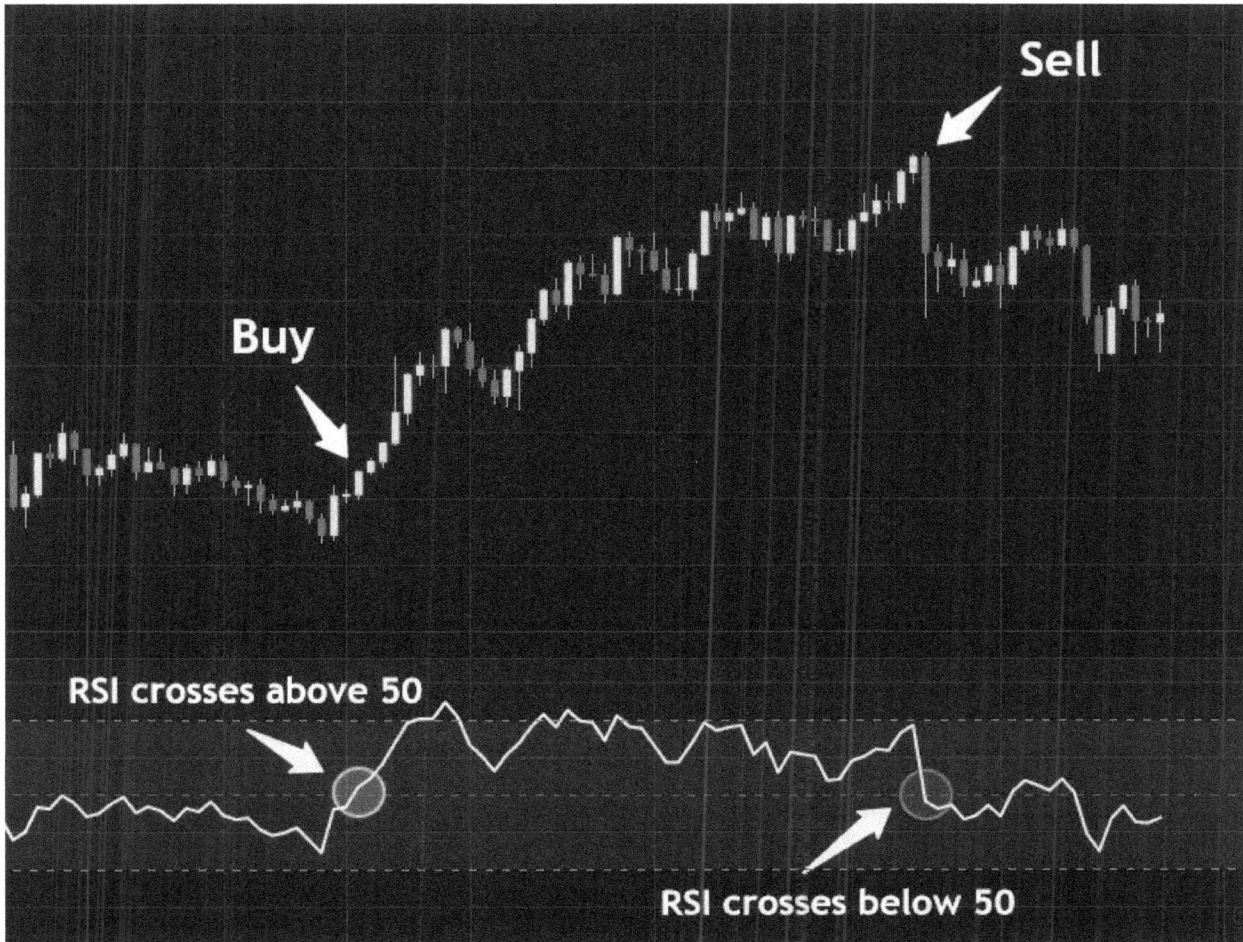

Example of a momentum trading strategy using the RSI

Trend Trading:

Trend trading strategies involve identifying and riding the wave of a particular trend in the market. This can be a lucrative strategy if done correctly.

There are two types of trends: up trends, and down trends. An up trend is when the price of an asset is moving higher over time. This is usually represented by a series of higher highs and higher lows on a price chart.

A down trend is just the opposite, with the price moving lower over time. This is usually represented by a series of lower highs and lower lows on a price chart.

The key to successful trend trading is to identify the type of trend that is currently happening in the market, and then trade in that direction.

For example, if you see an up trend, you would want to buy assets that are currently going up in value and ride the trend until it reverses. When it reverses you would sell those assets and look for another up trend to ride.

The same is true for down trends.

But at its core, trend trading is all about identifying the current direction of the market and then taking a position accordingly.

Important Rules to Follow To Increase Your Win Rate

Rule #1: Have a Trading Plan

This is probably the most important rule of them all. You need to have a trading plan before you enter any trade. Your trading plan should include:

-Your entry and exit conditions

-The stop loss levels for each trade

-How much you're risking on each trade

-What indicators you're using to make your decision

-When to take profits

If you don't have a trading plan, then it's very likely that you'll end up losing money.

Rule #2: Trade with the Trend

The markets tend to move in cycles, and it's important to identify which phase of the cycle the market is currently in. Is it in a bullish or bearish phase?

If you're not sure, then you can use technical indicators like moving averages to help you out. If the market is above the 200 EMA, then it's likely in a long-term uptrend. And if the market is below the 200 EMA, then it's likely in a long-term downtrend.

Once you've identified the trend, make sure to trade in that direction.

Rule #3: Don't Make Emotional Decisions When Trading

One of the biggest mistakes that traders make is trading based on emotions.

When you're emotional, you'll start making bad decisions that can cost you a lot of money.

The best way to avoid this is to have a plan and stick to it. Don't let your emotions get in the way of making rational decisions. If you find you are having trouble controlling your emotions you can create a trading bot that will trade for you automatically and remove emotions from the equation.

Rule #4: Backtest Your Strategies

This is a very important step that many traders skip. Backtesting is using your strategy on historical market data, this will show you how your strategy would have performed in the past. You can backtest manually or use software like TradingView to do it automatically.

It is also a good idea to test your strategy on a practice account without using real money. This is known as "papertrading", this is a good way to help you to identify any potential flaws in your strategy and make the necessary adjustments.

Rule 5: Manage Your Risk

The final rule is to make sure you are managing your risk properly. A good way to manage risk is to only trade with a small percentage of your total account balance (usually no more than five percent). This way if a trade goes against you, it won't wipe out your account.

Another way to manage risk is to use risk to reward ratios, this is when you set a stop loss level that is slightly below your entry price, and then target a profit level that is two or three times greater than your original stop loss.

These are just some of the rules that you need to follow if you want to be successful day trading crypto. By following these simple rules, you'll be well on your way to making consistent profits.

Chapter 2: How to Find High Probability Setups

The key to success with these strategies is finding high-probability setups and entering the trade with a positive risk-to-reward ratio. This means that your potential profits should be significantly higher than your potential losses.

Steps for Finding a High Probability Setup

A high probability set up should have multiple factors working in its favor, including:

- A well-defined trend

- Strong momentum

- Price is at a key support/resistance level

- Clear Entry signals

- Good risk-to-reward ratio

Step 1: Identify The Market Trend

The first step is to identify the trend. The trend is your friend, and it is important to trade with the trend whenever possible. There are three main types of trends: up, down, and sideways

Up Trend - A market that is trending higher is said to be in an up trend. The trendlines will slope upwards, and the price will make higher highs and higher lows

Down Trend - A market that is trending lower is said to be in a down trend. The trendlines will slope downwards, and the price will make lower highs and lower lows

Sideways - A market that is moving sideways is said to be in a consolidation phase. The trendlines will be horizontal, and the price will make higher highs and lower lows.

Once you have identified the trend, you need determine it's strength, and if it's likely to reverse soon.

Step 2: Look For Momentum

In order to scalp or day trade, you need to find stocks or currencies that are moving strongly in one direction. You can do this by looking for stocks or currencies that have strong momentum. This means that the price is moving quickly in one direction, with little or no pullback.

You can use these indicators to help you measure momentum and changes in momentum:

- The Relative Strength Index (RSI)

- The Moving Average Convergence/Divergence (MACD)

- The Stochastic Oscillator

Step 3: Trade Around Key Support/Resistance Levels

One of the most important factors to look for when day trading is a stock or currency that is nearing a key support or resistance level. A support level is a price level where buyers are expected to step in and prop up the price. A resistance level is a price level where sellers are expected to step in and push the price lower.

When price reaches a key support or resistance level, it often results in a reaction. The price will either breakout of the level, or reverse and move in the opposite direction. This makes it a high-probability setup for a trade.

Step 4: A Clear Entry Signal

Another important factor to look for is a clear entry signal. This means that the stock or currency has given you a clear indication that it is ready to breakout or reverse.

There are many different types of entry signals, but some of the most common ones are:

- Price Crossing a Moving Average - When the price crosses a moving average, it often signals a change in trend and is a good entry signal.

- Candlestick Patterns - There are many different candlestick patterns that can provide an entry signal, such as pin bars, doji , and engulfing candles.

- Bollinger Bands - The bands will tighten up or expand when the price is getting ready to breakout. This can provide an entry signal.

- Oscillators - Oscillators such as the RSI, MACD, and Stochastic Oscillator can give you an indication of when a stock or currency is overbought or oversold, and is ready to reverse direction.

Step 5:The Trade Has a Good Risk-to-Reward Ratio

One of the most important factors to look for when day trading is a good risk-to-reward ratio. This means that your potential profits should be significantly higher than your potential losses. A good risk-to-reward ratio should be at least 2:1, meaning that for every $1 you risk, you should be able to make at least $2 in profits.

Now that you know what to look for, let's take a look at some specific day trading and scalping strategies.

Chapter 3: High Probability Entry and Exit Signals Using Oscillators

Oscillators are a staple of technical analysis, and for good reason. They can be used to generate exit and entry signals, helping to improve your trading results. In this chapter, we'll take a look at some of the most reliable oscillator signals and how you can use them in your own trading.

Oscillators are technical indicators that help identify overbought or oversold conditions in the market, as well as possible reversal points. In this guide we will cover the most accurate entry and exit signals using oscillators.

When using entry/exit signals from oscillators, the first step is to identify the trend. This is because the signals that are produced will be much more reliable when taking signals that are in the direction of the trend. This means that if the market is in an uptrend, we will be looking for bullish signals (that indicate a buy). On the other hand, if the market is in a downtrend, we will be looking for bearish signals (that indicate a sell).

These signals should also be using in conjunction with support and resistance levels, as these can act as areas where the market may reverse.

In this chapter, we'll take a look at some of the most profitable technical indicators and explore how you can use them to generate trading signals.

To find these indicators on TradingView:

- Go into the "Indicators & Strategies" window on

- Click on the "Community Scripts" tab.

- Type the name of the indicator in the search box

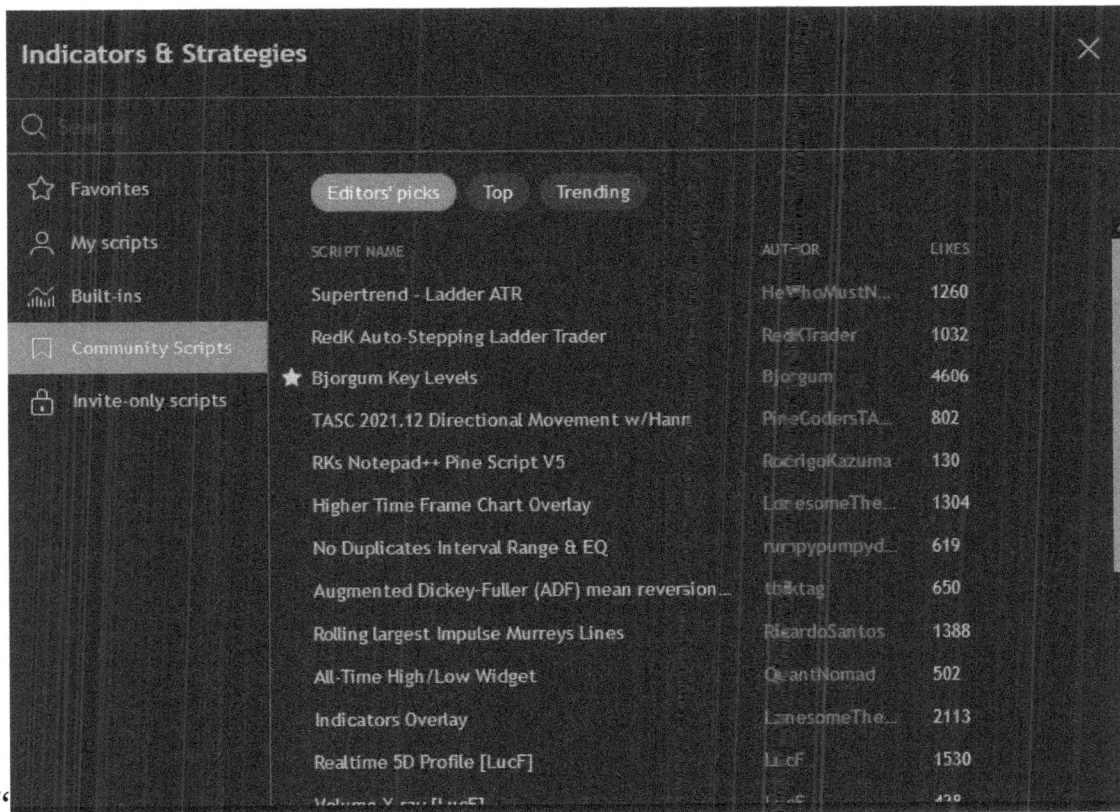

These indicators provide very accurate buy and sell signals, and are great for combining into a trading strategy.

Many of the signals in this chapter are from indicators that the TradingView community has created.

Entry/Exit Signal #1: RSI Wave Signals

Author: bartua

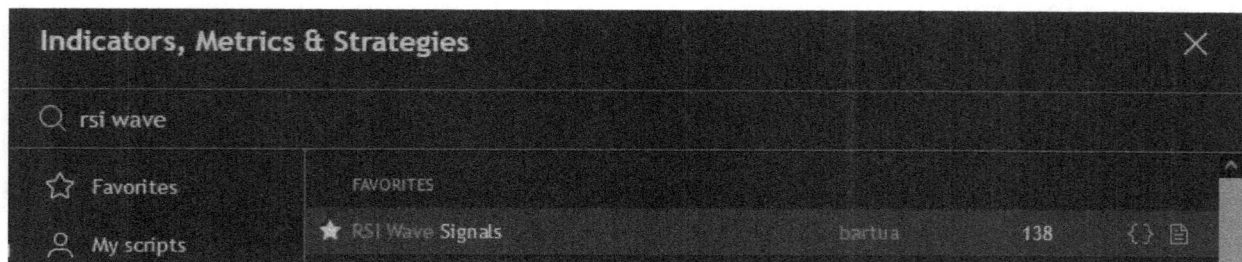

Search "RSI Wave Signals" in the indicator search box on TradingView to find this indicator (author – bartua)

How It Works:

This indicator is based on a modified RSI and is combined with a optimized trend tracker (OTT) moving average. Signals are generated when the moving average crosses above or below the moving average.

Tip:

- This indicator works best on shorter timeframes (5 min timeframe and lower)

Buy Signal:

- The RSI is oversold (below 1040) and crosses above the moving average (white line)

Sell Signal:

- The RSI is overbought (above 1060) and crosses below the moving average (white line)

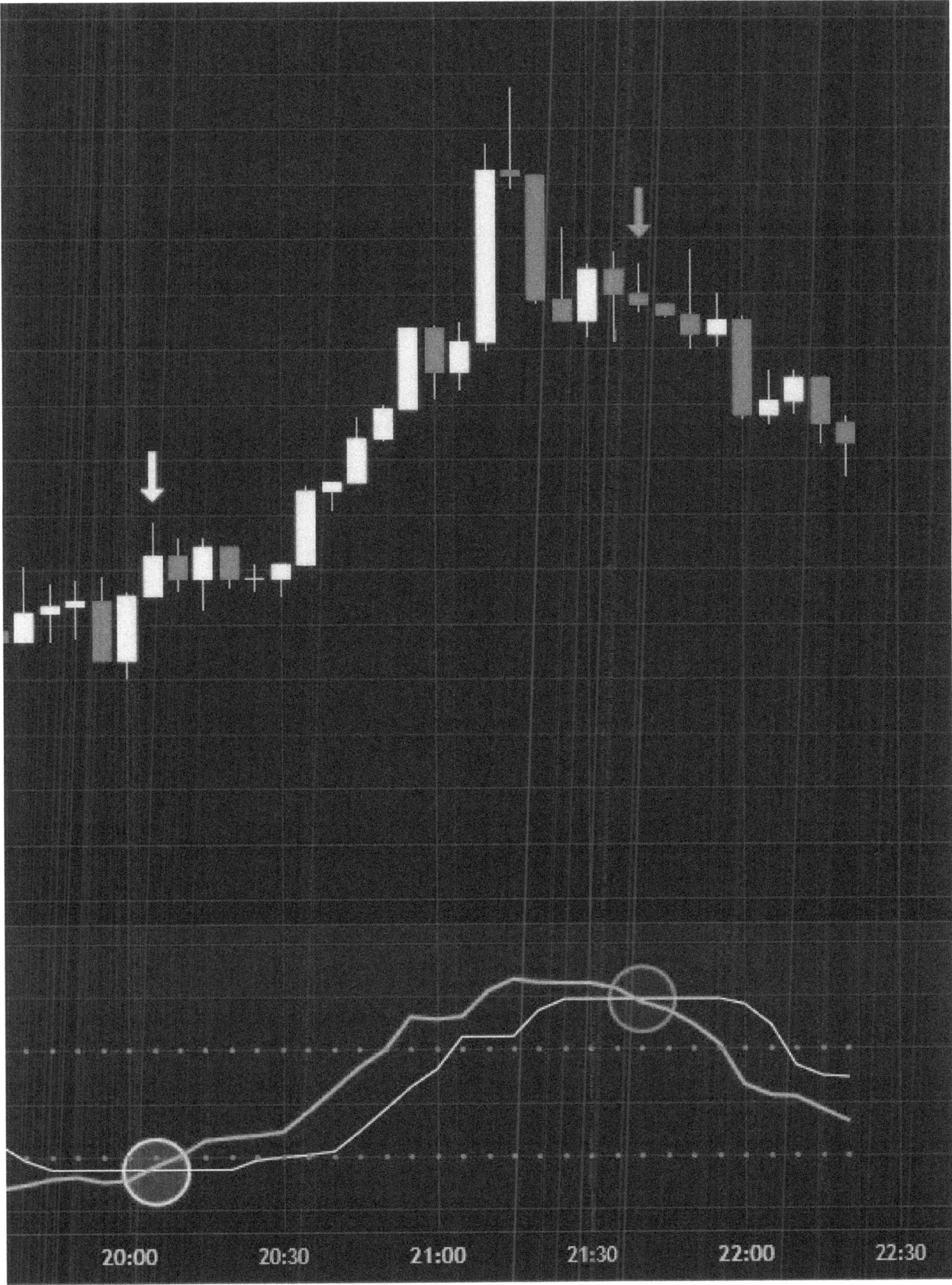

Example of buy and sell signals using this indicator

Entry/Exit Signal #2: RSI Center Line Cross

How it works:

This signal occurs when the RSI crosses above or below the 50 level, this is sometime refered to as a "center line cross" signal. When the RSI crosses 50, this indicates a trend change is occurring.

If the RSI crosses above 50 this is a bullish signal and suggests prices are likely to continue to move higher.

Conversely, if the RSI crosses below 50 this is a bearish signal and indicates prices are likely to move lower.

50 level cross signals work best in trending markets but can also be used in rangebound or sideways moving markets.

Tip:
- Change the length to 30 for swing trading signals

Buy Signal:
- When the RSI crosses above 50

Sell Signal:
- When the RSI crosses below 50

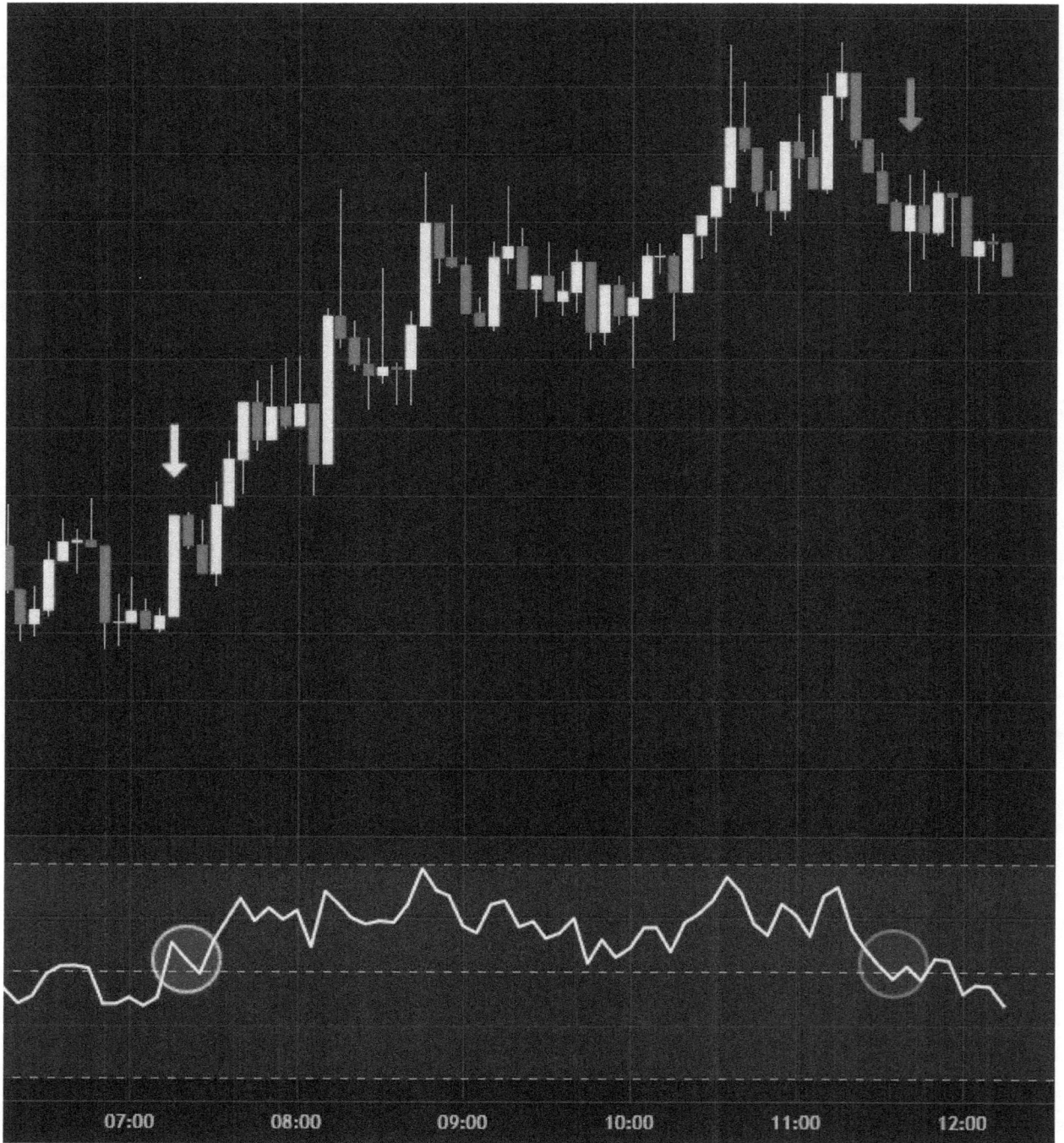

Example of buy and sell signals using this RSI signal

Entry/Exit Signal 3: Bjorgum TSI

Author: Bjorgum

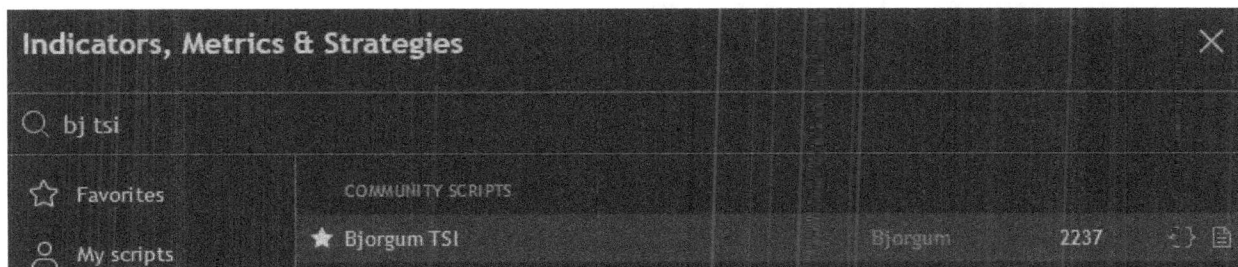

Search "Bjorgum TSI" in the indicator search box on TradingView to find this indicator (author – Bjorgum)

How it Works:

This is a version of the TSI (true strength indicator) and is a crossover oscillator with two lines, one fast and one slow.

Signals are generated when the fast line crosses above or below the slow line.

Tip: To get fewer whipsaw signals you can change the TSI speed to slow in the indicator settings

Buy Signal:

- The fast line (TSI value line) crosses above the slow line (TSI signal line)
- TSI will turn blue

Sell Signal:

- The fast line (TSI value line) crosses below the (TSI signal line)
- TSI will turn red

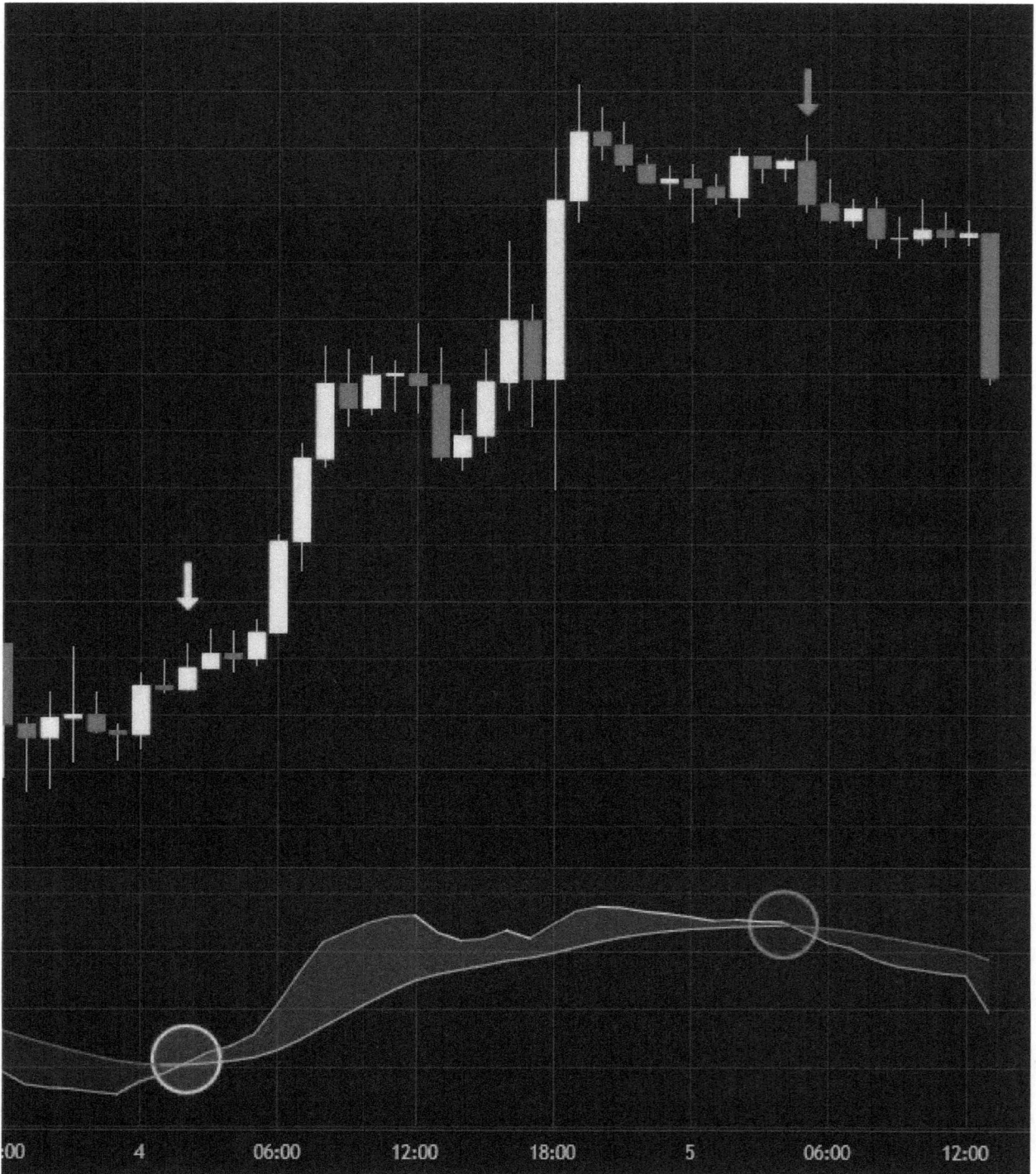

Example of a buy and sell signal using this indicator

Entry/Exit Signal #4: Scalp Pro

Author: ovelix

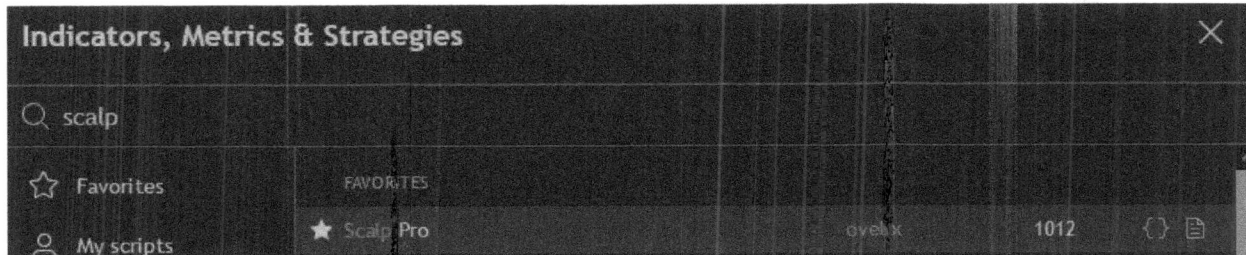

Search "Scalp Pro" in the indicator search box on TradingView to find this indicator (author – ovelix)

How it Works:

This indicator is based on modified MACD calculations and is displayed as a crossover oscillator with two lines, one fast and one slow (similar to a stochastic). Signals are generated when the fast line crosses above or below the slow line.

This indicator is great for scalping, it produces frequent signals most of which are accurate. The buy and sell signals will appear as labels on this indicator making it easy to use. This indicator works well in volatile market conditions.

Tip:
- Change the smooth length to 10 to reduce the amount of false signals

Buy Signal:
- The fast line crosses above the slow line and a green buy label appears

Sell Signal:
- The fast line crosses below the slow line and a red sell label appears

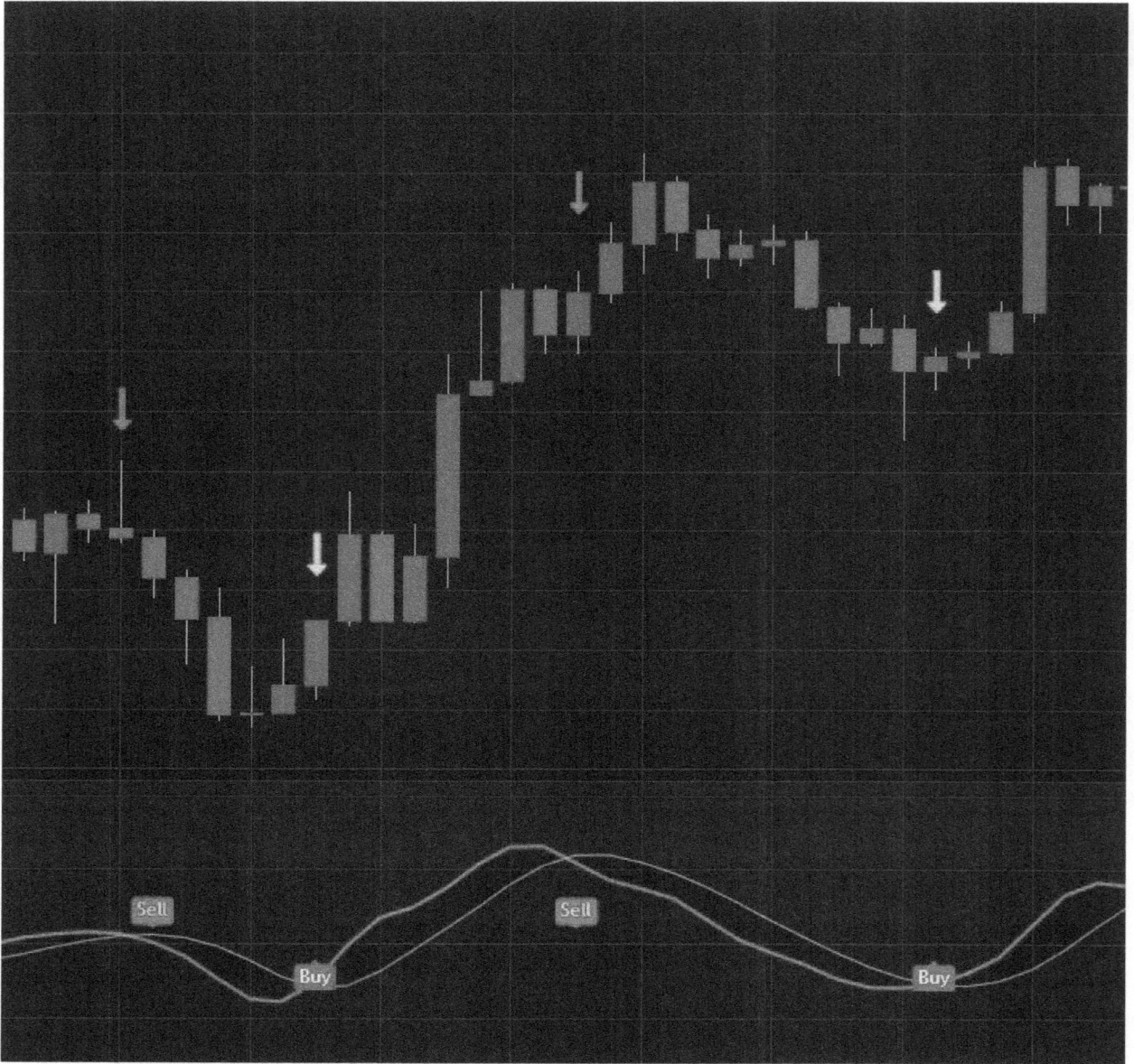

Example of buy and sell signals using this indicator

Entry/Exit Signal #5: RSI Trend Line Break

How it works:

Trend lines can be drawn on the RSI indicator to identify potential buy and sell signals. When the RSI crosses above a trend line, it generates a buy signal. When the RSI crosses below a trend line, it generates a sell signal.

Typically a trend line will break on the RSI before a trend reversal occurs in the market, this makes it a good leading indicator signal.

Tip:

- Change RSI length to 21

Buy Signal:

- The buy signal is generated when the RSI crosses above a downtrend line. This indicates that momentum is shifting to the upside and prices are likely to reverse higher.

Sell Signal:

- The sell signal is generated when the RSI crosses below an uptrend line. This indicates that momentum is shifting to the downside and prices are likely to reverse lower.

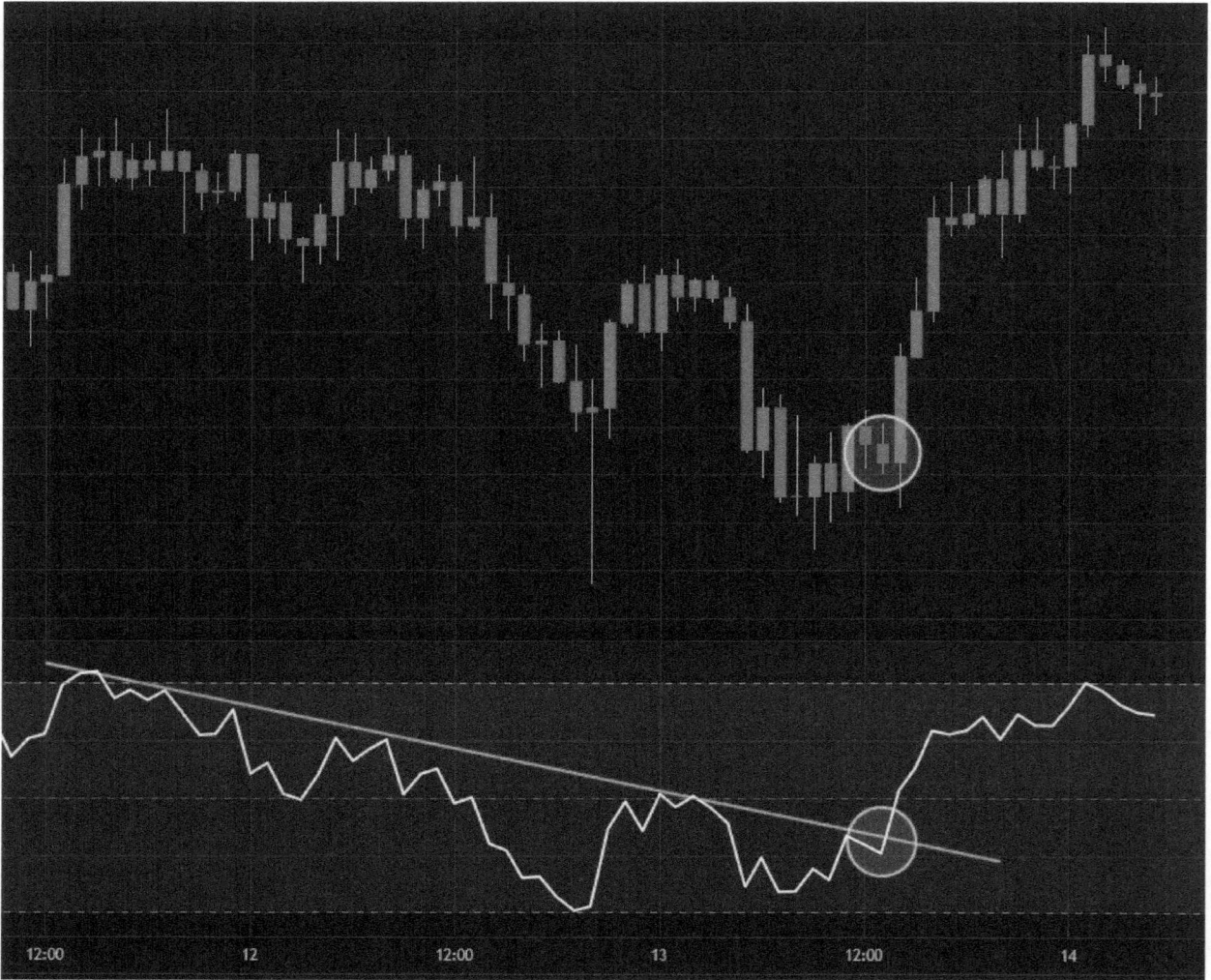

Example of a buy signal (green circle) using this method

Entry/Exit Signal #6: MACD (improved settings)

What Is It?

This method uses the MACD indicator crossovers as buy/sell signals. The MACD is a momentum indicator that is based on two exponential moving averages.

This strategy changes the default settings of the MACD to produce more accurate buy/sell signals and filter out the bad signals that frequently occur with the default MACD settings.

Change the MACD setting to:

- Fast Length = 20, Slow Length = 50, Signal Smoothing = 21

Buy Signal:

- The fast MACD line crosses above the slow line

Sell Signal:

- The fast MACD line crosses below the slow line

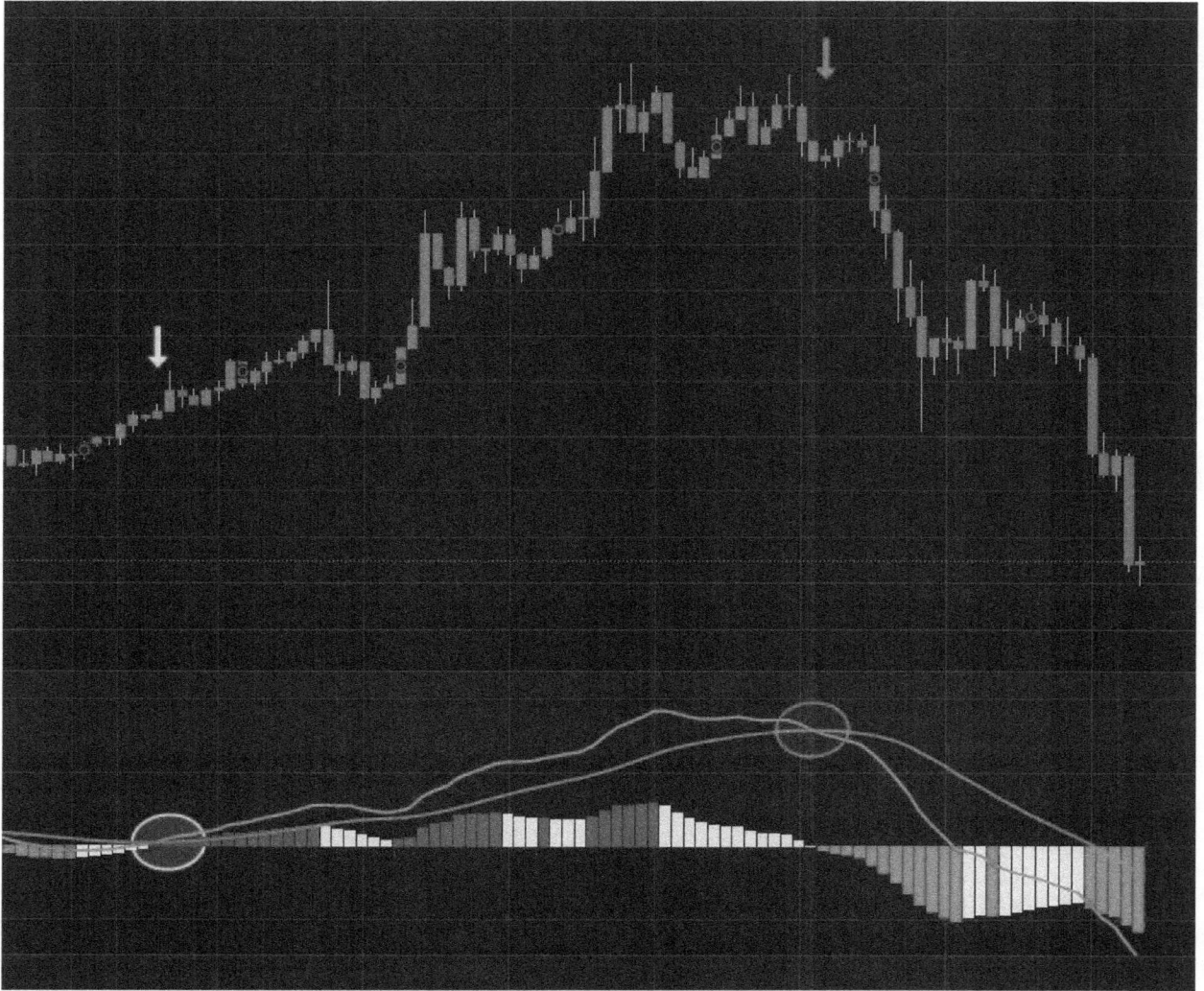

Example of buy and sell signals using this indicator

Entry/Exit Signal #7: RSI + Moving Average Cross

How it works:

The RSI indicator is combined with a moving average to create a trading signal. When the RSI crosses above the moving average, it generates a buy signal. When the RSI crosses below the moving average, it generates a sell signal.

The moving average helps to filter out noise and provides a smoother representation of price action. The RSI is used to identify momentum. When the two indicators are combined, they can provide accurate buy and sell signals in any market conditions.

Tip:

- Use a 21 EMA (exponential moving average) or 20 VWMA(volume weighted moving average)

Buy Signal:

- The buy signal is generated when the RSI crosses above the moving average. This indicates that momentum is shifting to the upside and prices are likely to continue higher.

Sell Signal:

- The sell signal is generated when the RSI crosses below the moving average. This indicates that momentum is shifting to the downside and prices are likely to continue lower.

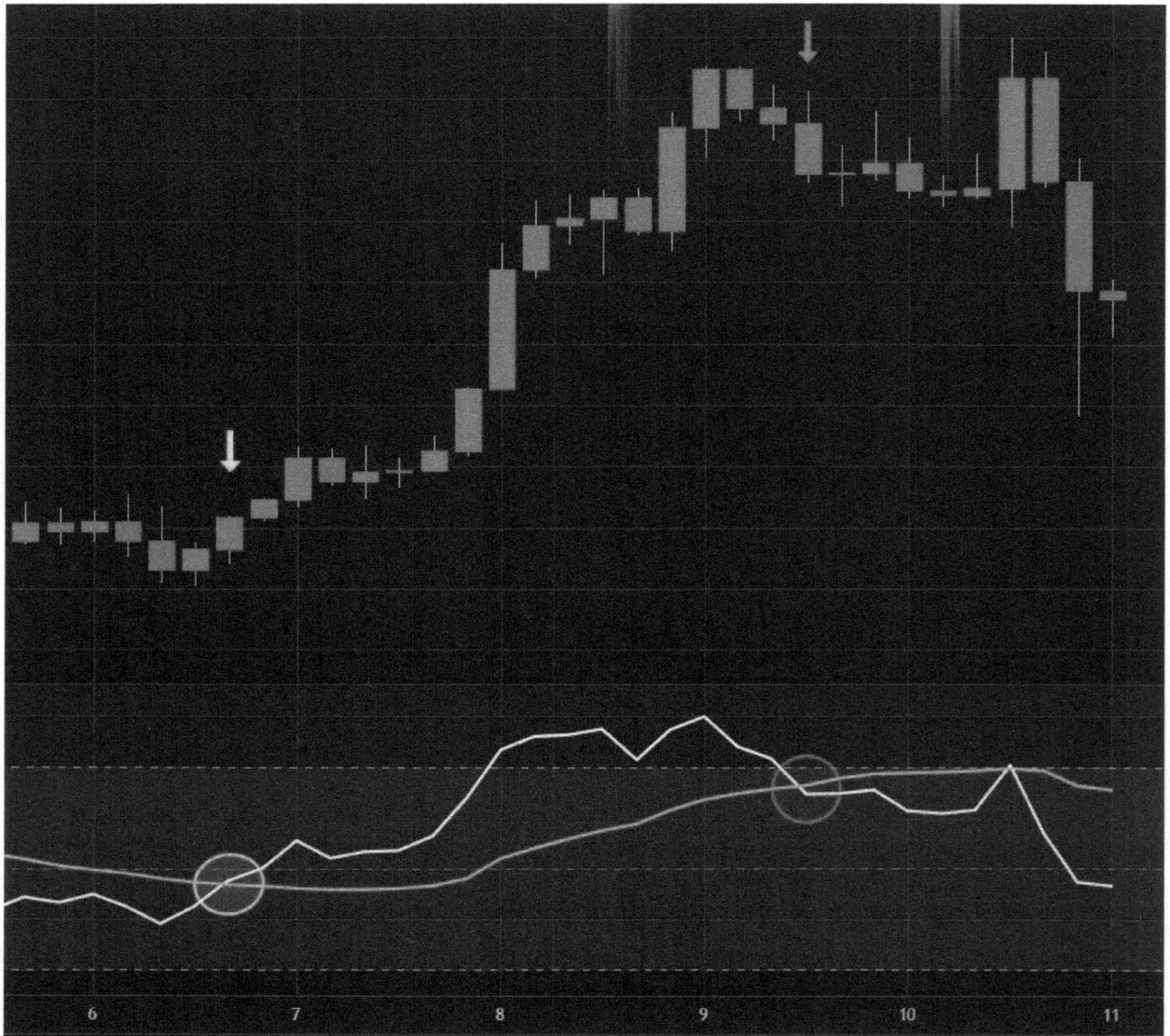

Example of buy (green circle) and sell (red circle) signals using this strategy

Entry/Exit Signal #8: Stochastic Weights - Basic

To find this indicator type in "Stochastic Weights - Basic", in the indicator search box on TradingView (author - BigBitsIO

How it works:

This indicator is similar to a normal stochastics with a %K and %D line. When the stochastic moves above 80 it is considered overbought and below 20 is oversold. This indicator can give more accurate signals then a regular stochastic since it includes other values in its calculations.

Tip: enable all of the stochastics in the indicator settings

Buy Signal:

- The %K line crosses above the %D line while under 50

Or

- The stochastic above 20 after being oversold

Sell Signal:

- The %K line crosses below the %D line while above 50

Or

- The stochastic crosses below 80 after being oversold

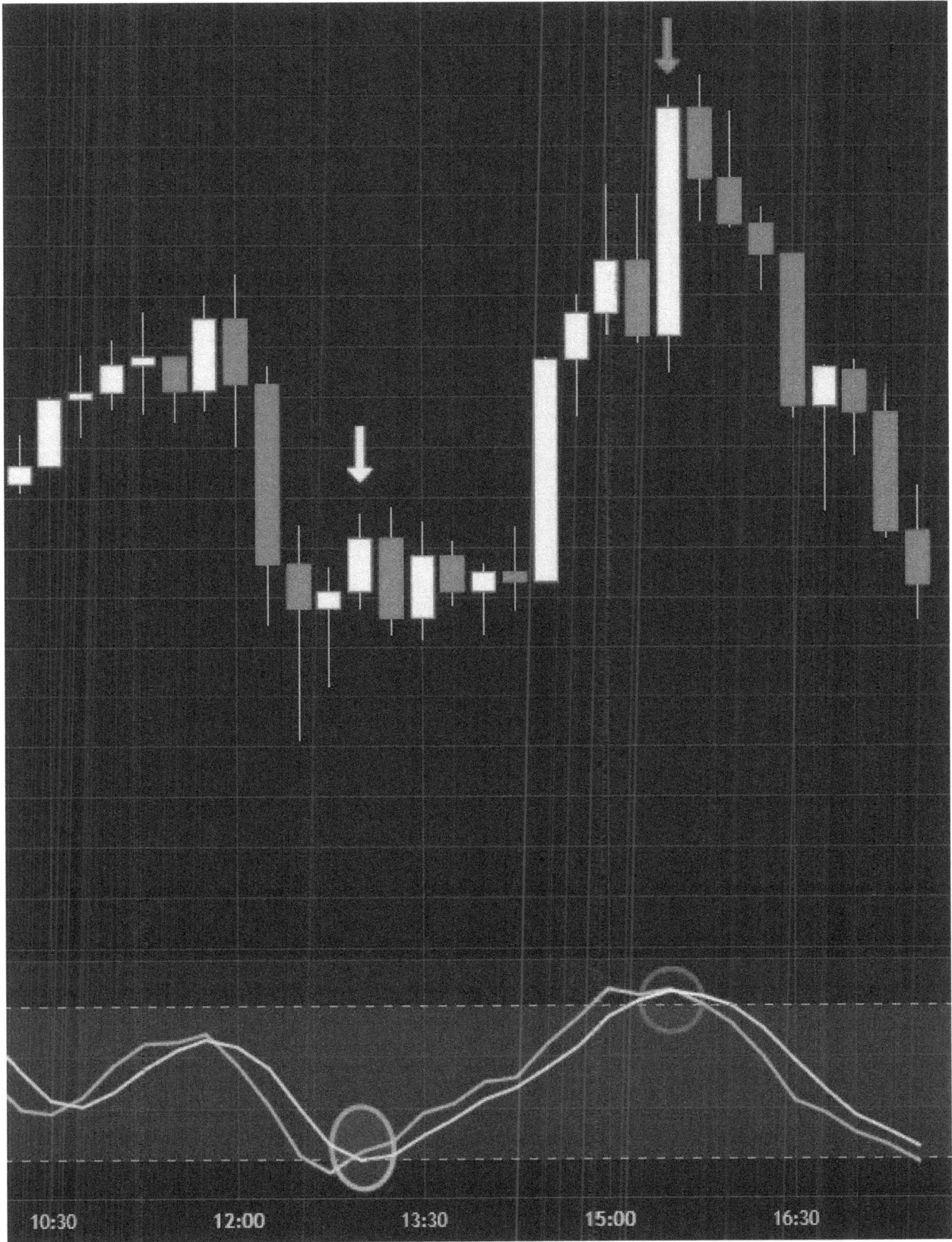

Example of buy and sell signals using this indicator

Entry/Exit Signal #9: Normalized Smoothed MACD

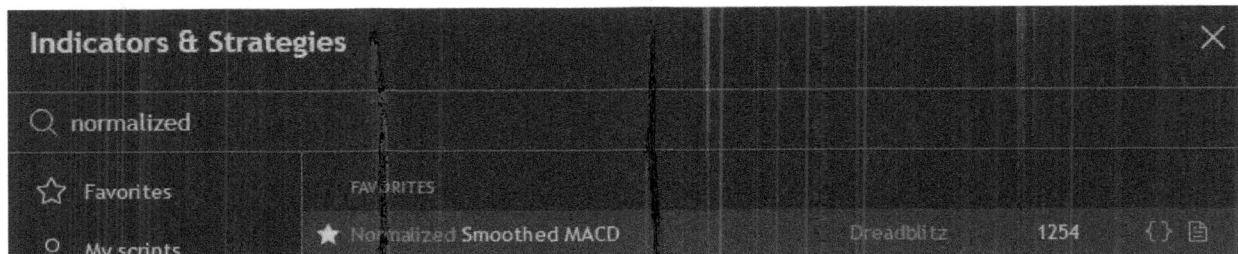

Search "Normalized Smoothed MACD" in the indicator search box on TradingView to find this indicator (author – Dreadblitz)

What is it?

This indicator is an improved version of the MACD indicator, and provides more reliable entry and exit signals then a regular MACD. Two lines are displayed on this indicator, the signal line and MACD line

Buy/Long Signal:

- The MACD line is below the zero line

- The MACD crosses above the signal line and the MACD line turns green

Sell/Short Signal:

- The MACD line is above the zero line and turns red

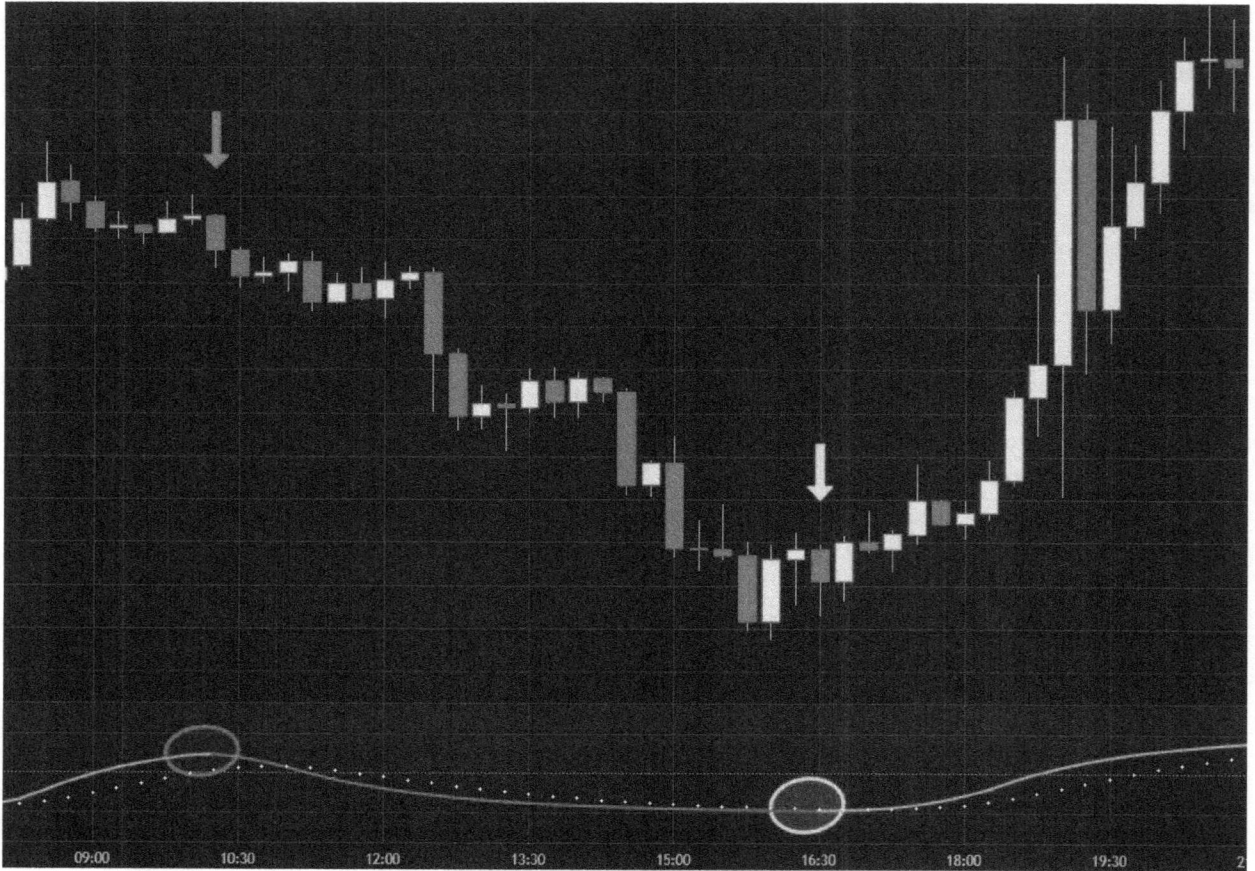

Example of entry and exit signals using this indicator

Entry/Exit Signal #10: Quantitative Qualitative Estimation QQE

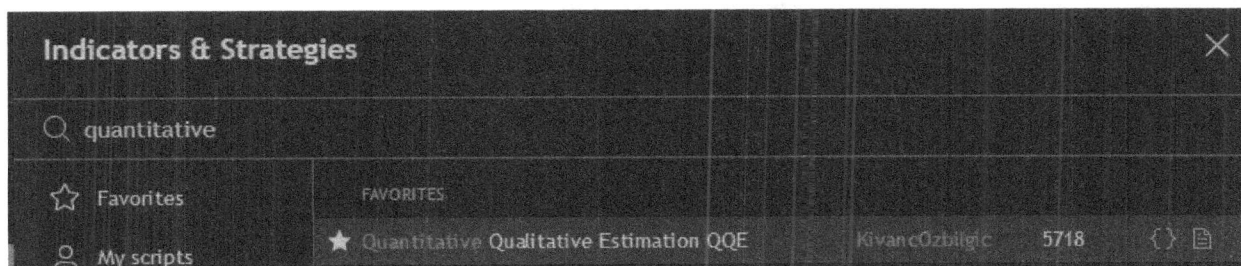

Search "Quantitative Qualitative Estimation" in the indicator search box on TradingView to find this indicator (author – KivancOzbilgic)

What is it?

This indicator combines the RSI with the two ATR lines, when the ATR lines cross this provides buy and sell signals. This indicator will display buy and sell signals on it making it easy to use.

You can also use overbought and oversold levels on this indicator for signals with below 30 being oversold and above 70 being overbought.

Buy Signal:
- When the fast line crosses above the slower line

Sell Signal
- When the fast line crosses below the slow line

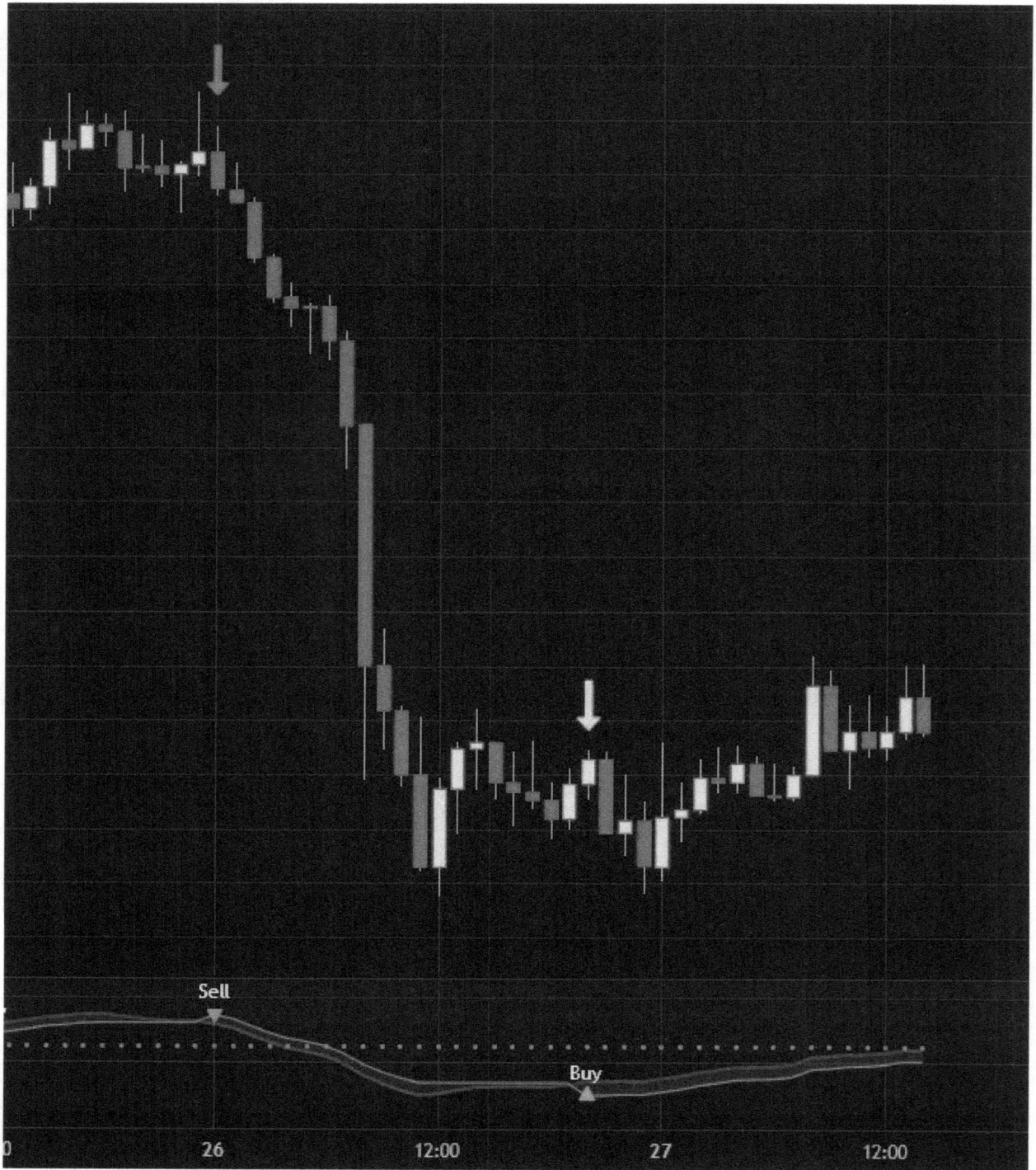

Example of buy and sell signals using this indicator

Entry/Exit Signal #11: Stochastic OTT

Author: KivancOzbilgic

Search "Stochastic OTT" in the indicator search box on TradingView to find this indicator (author – KivancOzbilgic)

What is it?

This indicator is similar to the stochastic oscillator, but it combines the stochastic oscillator with the optimized trend tracker indicator. This reduces the false signals given by the stochastic oscillator that can be caused by volatile moves.

Tip:

Change the settings to:

%K Length = 100

%K Smoothing = 10

OTT period = 2

OTT percent = 0.5

Indicator Buy Signal:

- When the fast line crosses above the slow line

Indicator Sell Signal

- When the fast line crosses below the slow line

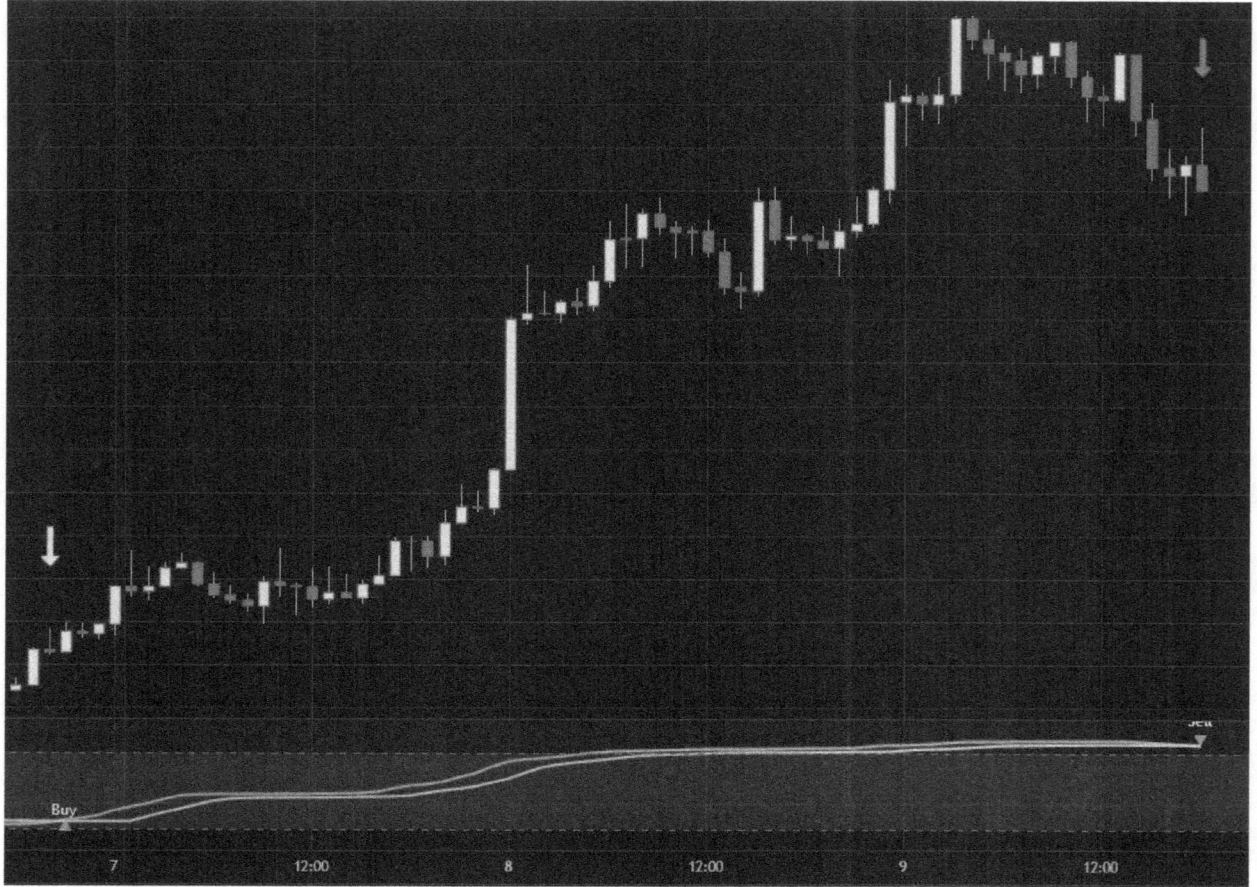

Example of buy and sell signals using this indicator

Entry/Exit Signal #12: Boom Hunter Pro

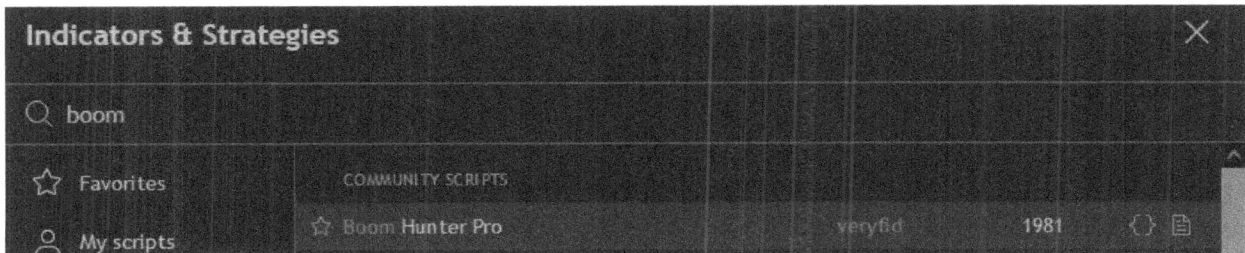

Search "Boom Hunter Pro" in the indicator search box on TradingView to find this indicator (Author – veryfid)

How it Works:

This is a oscillator displays two lines that cross over similar to a stochastic indicator but it uses a number of different calculations to produce overbought and oversold signals. This will display buy and sell signals as green and red dots.

Buy Signal:

- Green dots appear on the oscillator

Sell Signal:

- Red dots appear on the oscillator

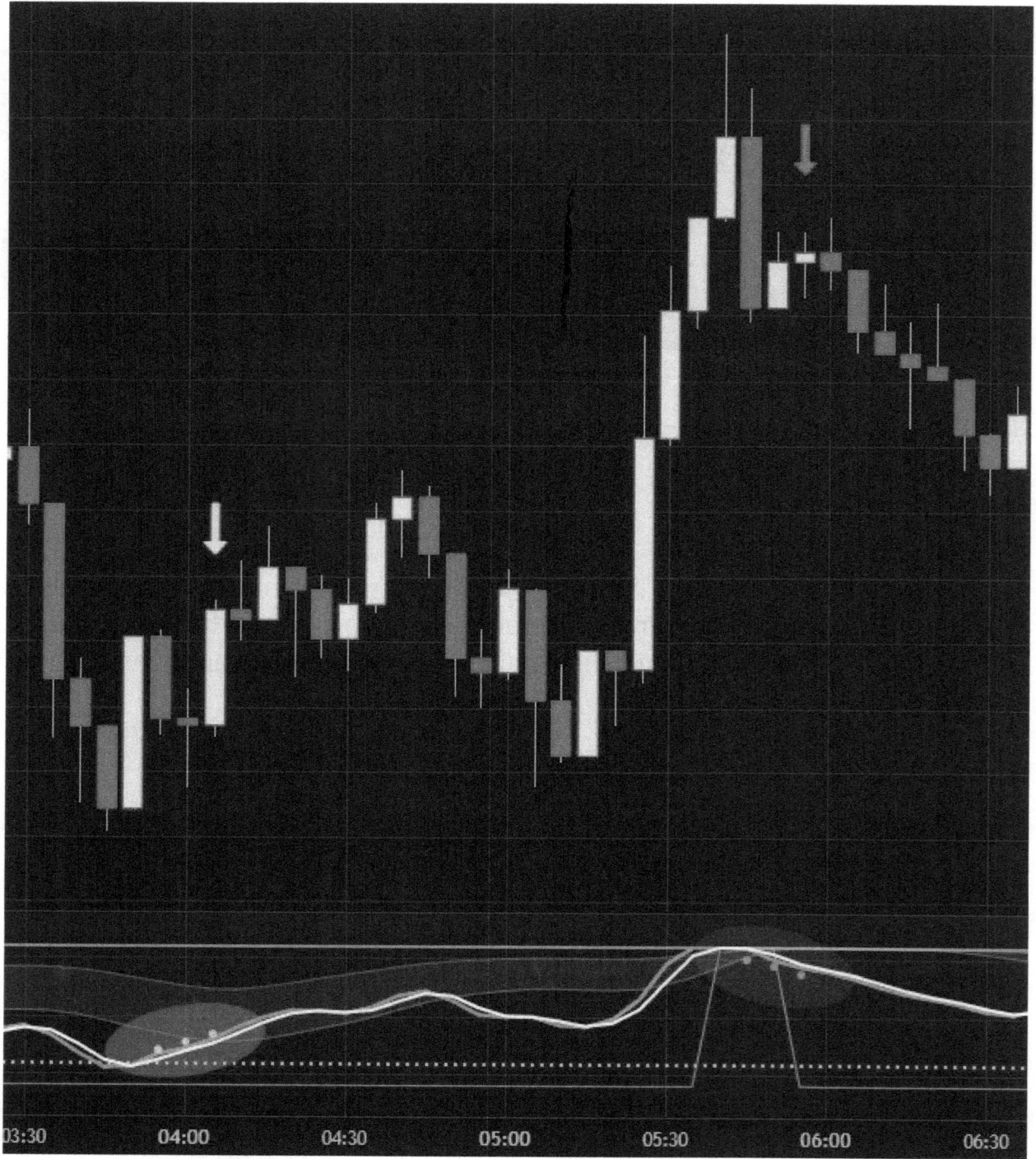

Example of buy signals (green circle) and sell signals (red circle) using the Boom Hunter Pro indicator

Chapter 4: High Win Rate Day Trading and Scalping Strategies

The strategies in this chapter are some of the best strategies I have used to make money in the markets over the years. These strategies are simple to follow and easy to use. However it is important that you use good risk management (stop losses) and papertrade these strategies on a practice account first before using real money. Make sure to only enter trades once all of the entry conditions are met, and avoid overtrading.

Tips for Using These Strategies

1. Look for market conditions that are in your favor

2. Use price action to find high probability trade setups

3. Trade with the trend whenever possible

4. Use indicators to help you time your entries and exits.

5. Stay disciplined and don't overtrade.

6. Always use a stop loss to protect your capital.

7. Have a trading plan and stick to it

8. Practice makes perfect, so paper trade before you start trading with real money.

Strategy #1: 100 SMA Scalping Strategy

Strategy Overview:

This is a scalping strategy that is based on taking bounces off of the 100 SMA. The 100 SMA will generally act as a strong support/resistance level (depending on the trend), and we will use the RSI as a confirmation indicator for entering.

When using this strategy take trades in the direction of the daily trend.

Step 1) Add the Indicators

For this strategy we will add three indicators on our chart:

- 100 MA (simple moving average)
- 500 MA
- 8 MA
- RSI – change length to 2

Step 2) Buy Conditions

Enter a trade only when all of the following rules are met:

- Candles are closing above the 500 MA
- Price is touching the 100 MA
- RSI crosses above 70
- Enter long trade when a candle closes above the 8 MA and 100 MA

Step 4) Sell Conditions

Close the trade or take profits if one of these conditions occurs:

- The RSI crosses below 30

Or

- A candle closes below the 8 MA

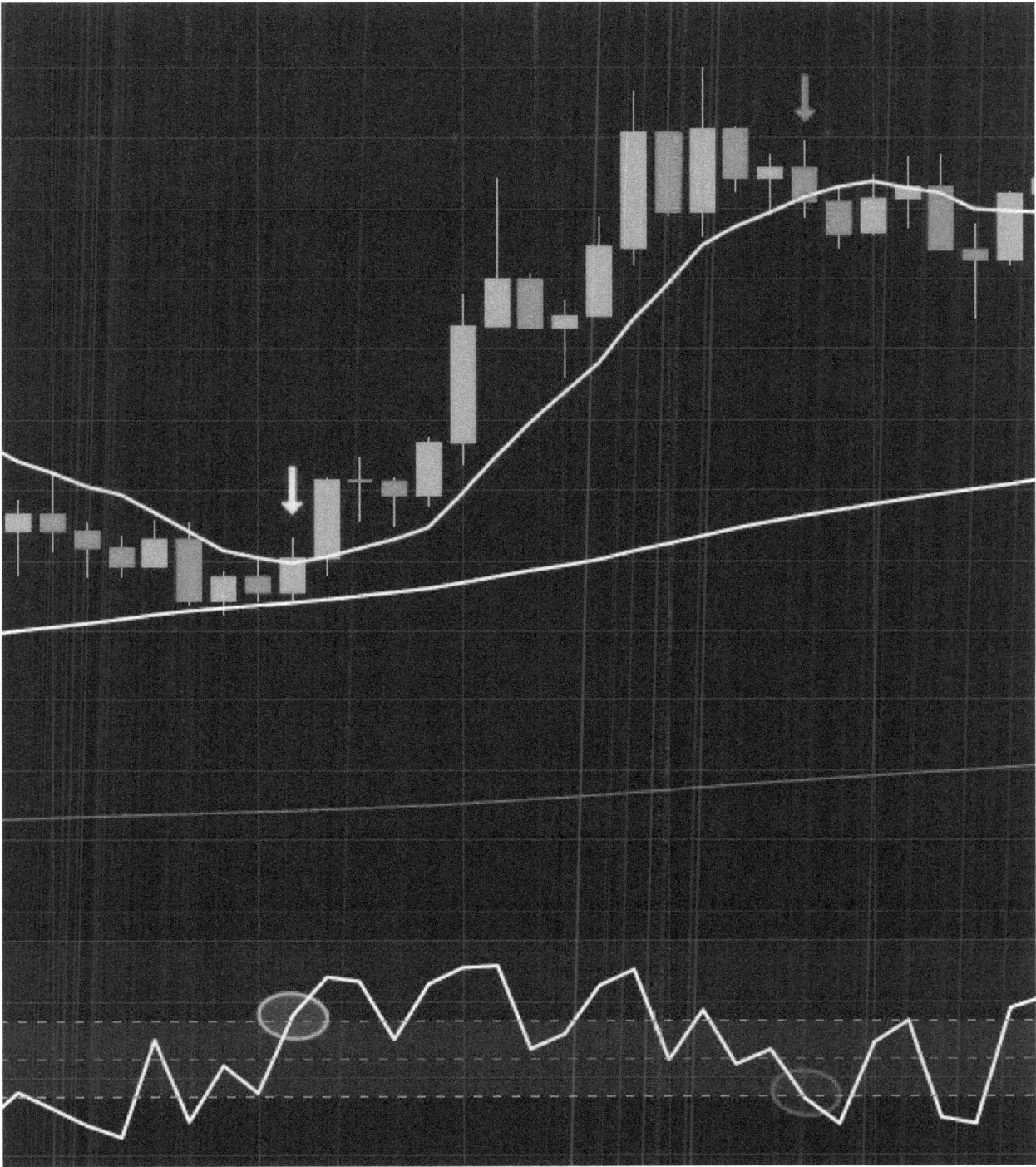

Example of a entry (green arrow) and exit (red arrow) using this strategy

Strategy #2: Schaff Trend Cycle Reversal Strategy

Strategy Overview:

- This is a trend reversal trading strategy designed for entering bottoms and selling/shorting tops

- This strategy uses a confluence of three different signals to identify market tops and bottoms

Step 1) Set up Your Chart

First draw a trend line -

- Draw a trend line connecting at least three swing highs or swing lows

Next add the following indicators:

- Schaff Trend Cycle (STC) – indicator by everget (community indicator on TradingView)

- 12 MA (simple moving average)

- 5 EMA (exponential moving average)

Step 2) Buy Conditions

Enter a trade only when all of the following rules are met:

- The STC crosses above 75 and turns green

- The 5 EMA crosses above the 12 MA

- Enter long trade when a candle closes above the trend line

- Place stop loss under the last swing low

Step 4) Sell Conditions

Close the trade or take profits if this signal occurs:

- The STC crosses below 75 (red dot will appear)

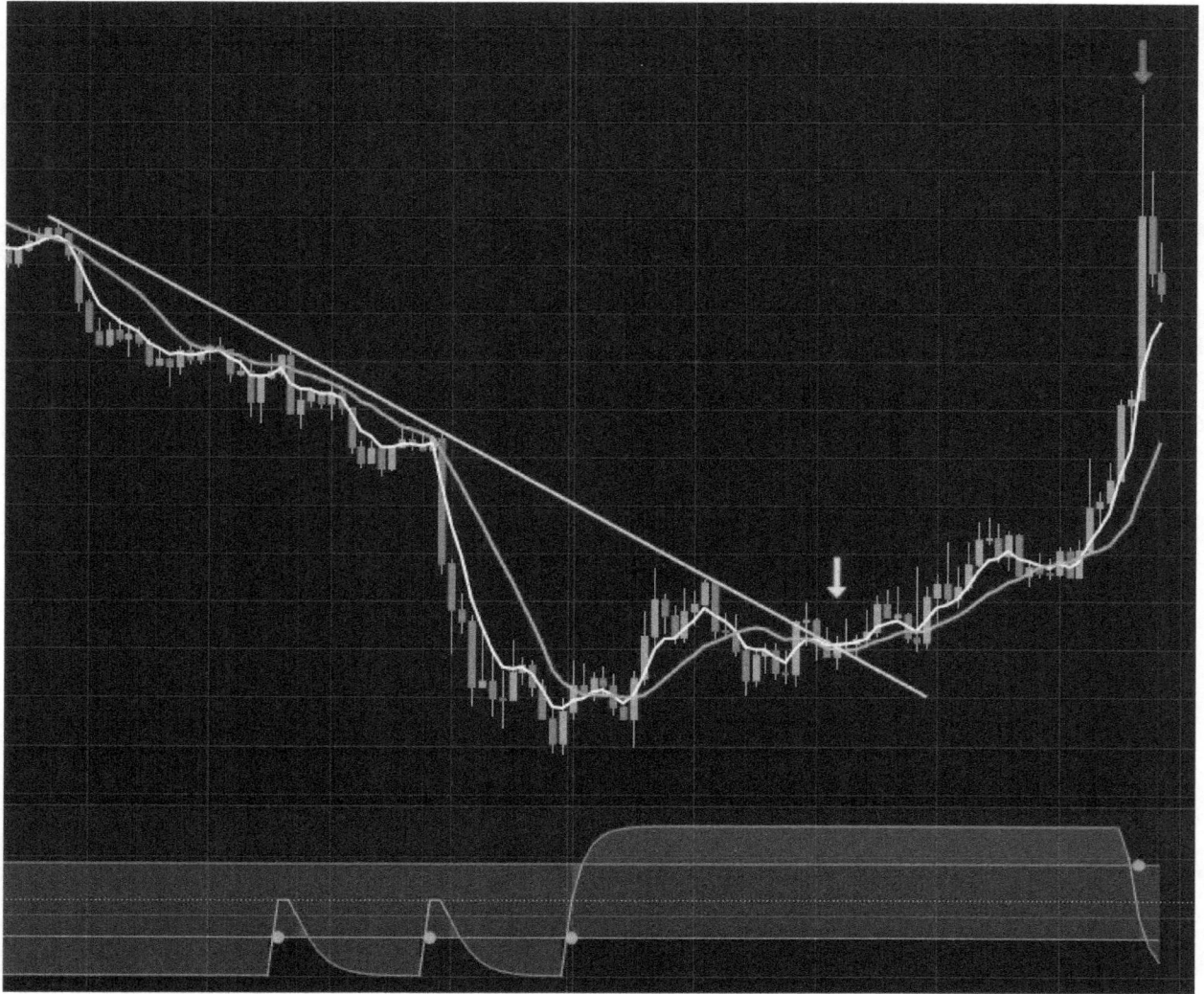

Example of a entry (green arrow) and exit (red arrow) using this strategy

Strategy #3: Support and Resistance Scalping Strategy

Strategy Overview:

- This strategy is based on trading horizontal support and resistance zones

- This strategy works best when the market is consolidating in a trading range (moving sideways)

Step 1) Add the Indicators

For this strategy we will add the following indicators on our chart:

- Normalized smoothed MACD (NSM) – indicator by Dreadblitz (TradingView community indicator)

- 30 HMA (hull moving average)

- SRchannel indicator (TradingView community indicator) by LonesomeTheBlue

Step 2) Buy Conditions

Enter a trade only when all of the following rules are met:

- The NSM is below 0 and turns green

- Price is touching or near the support level

- A candle closes above the HMA

Step 3) Sell Conditions

Close the trade or take profits if one of these conditions occurs:

- A candle closes below the HMA

- A candle touches the resistance zone

Example of a entry (green arrow) and exit (red arrow) using this strategy

Strategy #4: Simple "Buy the Dip Strategy"

Strategy Overview:

- This is a trend trading strategy designed to get you in emerging trends at a good price

- This strategy should be used for trending markets only

Step 1) Add the Indicators

For this strategy we will add the following indicators on our chart:

- 40 MA

- 10 MA

- RSI – change the length to 4

Step 2) Buy Conditions

Enter the trade only when all of these rules are met:

- The 10 MA crosses above the 40 MA

- The RSI crosses below 30

- Enter after the RSI crosses above 30 and a candle closes above the 40 MA

Step 3) Sell Conditions

Close the trade or take profits if one of these conditions occurs:

- A candle closes below the 40 MA

- The 10 MA crosses below the 40 MA

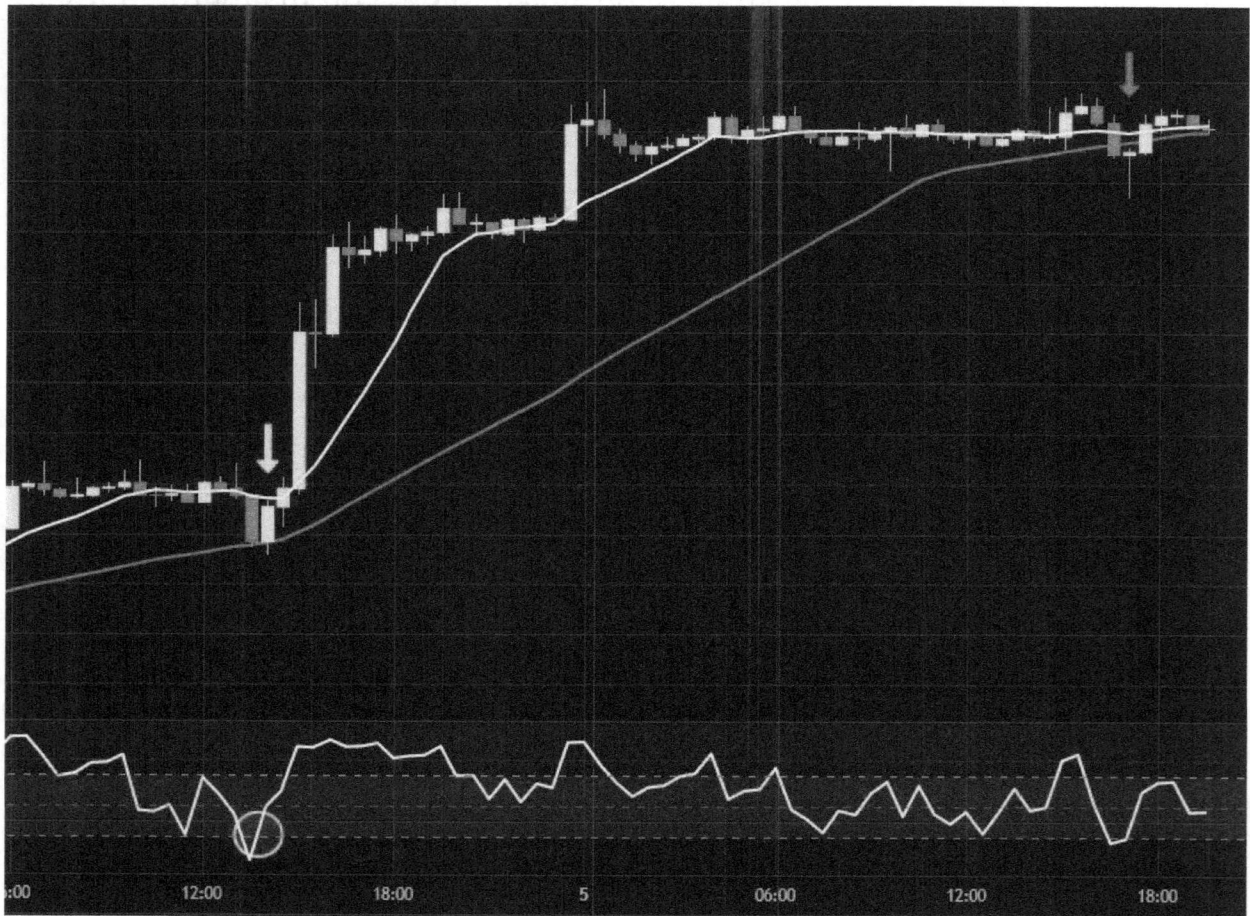

Example of a entry (green arrow) and exit (red arrow) using this strategy

Strategy #5: Double RSI Strategy

Strategy Overview:

In this strategy you will combine two RSI (relative strength index) indicators that are different lengths, entry/exit signals will occur when the two RSI's crossover. This strategy can be used for both scalping and day trading.

Step 1) Add the Indicators

For this strategy we will add three indicators on our chart:

- 30 HMA (Hull moving average)

- RSI – change length to 21

- RSI – change length to 5

  Move the two RSI's into the same window, it should look like the screenshot below.

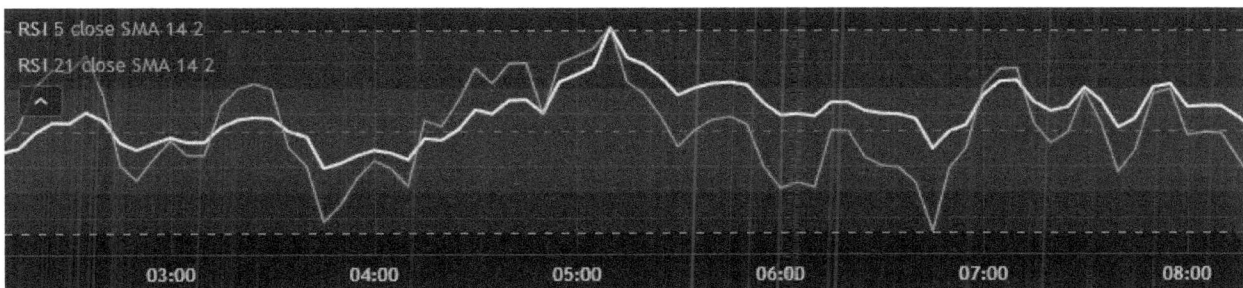

Step 2) Buy Conditions

Enter the trade only when all of these rules are met:

- The 5 period RSI crosses above the 21 period RSI

- Enter long trade on the next candle close above the 30 HMA (should not be more than 2 candles from the RSI crossover).

Step 3) Sell Conditions

Close the trade or take profits if one of these conditions occurs:

- A candle closes below the 30 HMA

- The 5 period RSI crosses below the 21 period RSI

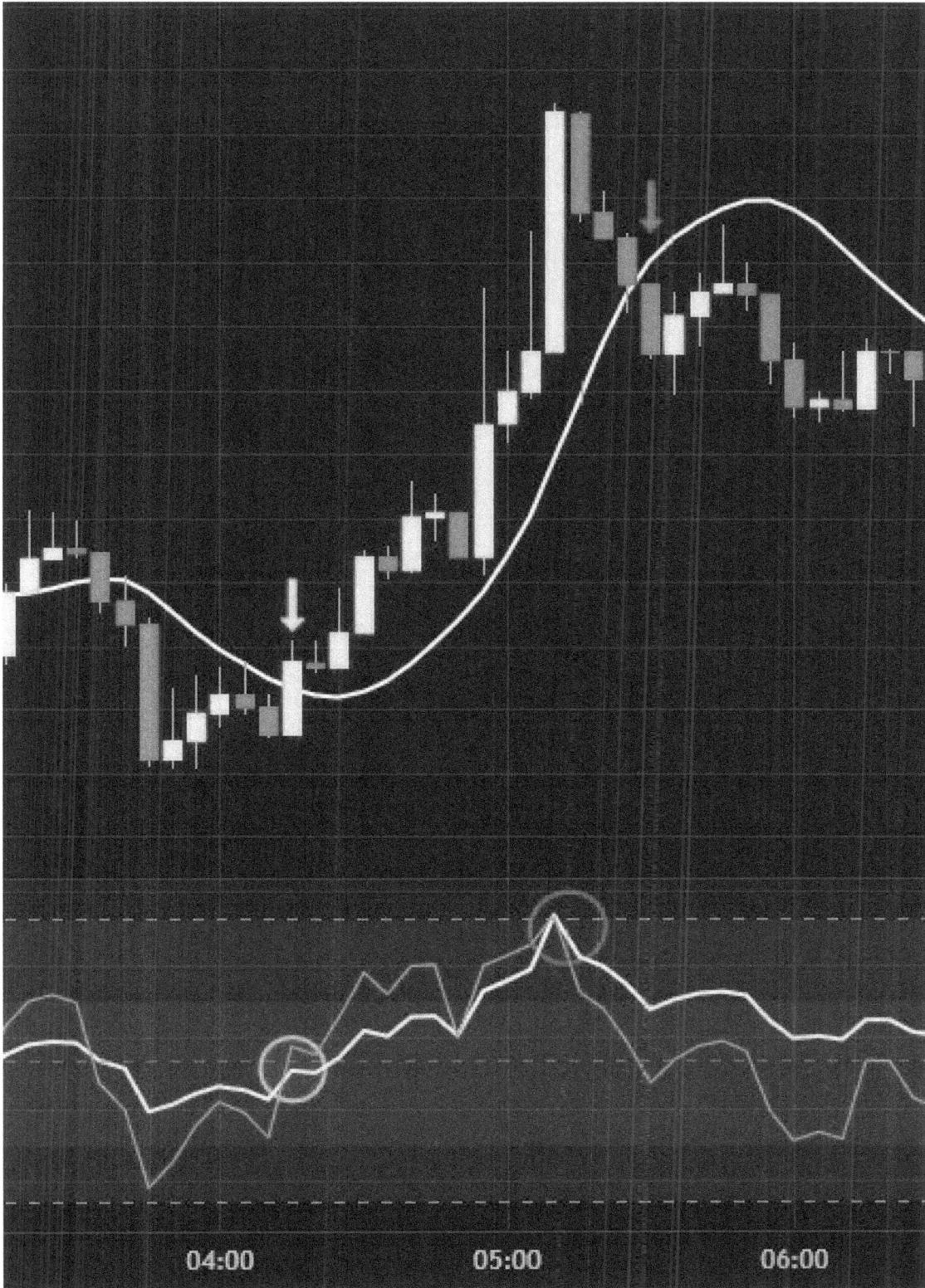

Example of a entry (green arrow) and exit (red arrow) using this strategy

Strategy #6: Bollinger Bands + Stochastic Scalping Strategy

Strategy Overview: This is a scalping strategy using the Bollinger bands and stochastic indicators. To get the best results when using this strategy trade in the direction of the daily trend.

Step 1) Add the Indicators

For this strategy we will add three indicators on our chart:

- Bollinger Bands with settings:

  Length = 20, Stdev = 2.5

- Stochastic with settings

  %K = 5, %K smooth = 3, %D = 3

Step 2) Buy Conditions

Enter the trade only when all of these rules are met:

- Price is touching or below the bottom Bollinger Band

- The stochastic is oversold (below 30)

- Buy when the stochastic crosses up

- Place stop loss under the low of the entry candle

Step 3) Sell Conditions

Close the trade or take profits if one of these conditions occurs:

- The stochastic is overbought (above 70)

- Price touches the middle Bollinger band line

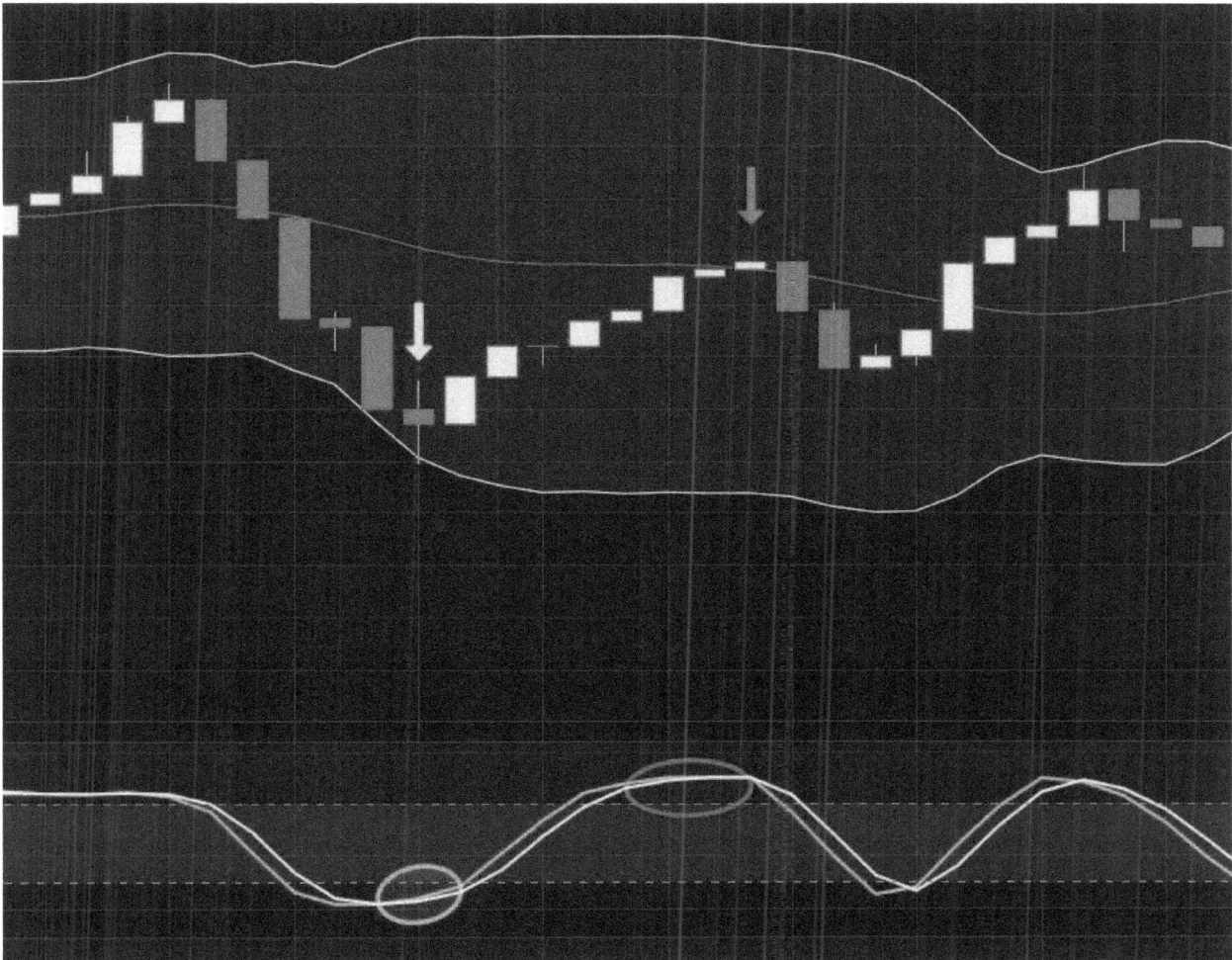

Example of a entry (green arrow) and exit (red arrow) when longing with this strategy

Strategy #7: HMA + RSI

Strategy Overview: This is a simple day trading strategy that uses the RSI for entries and exits. This is a good strategy for trading intraday trends.

Step 1) Add the Indicators

For this strategy we will add three indicators on our chart:

- RSI, set length to 30

- 40 period HMA (Hull moving average)

Step 2) Buy Conditions

Enter the trade only when all of these rules are met.

- Candles are closing above the HMA

- Buy when the RSI crosses above 50

- Place stop loss under the last swing low

Step 3) Sell Conditions

Close the trade or take profits if one of these conditions occurs:

- A candle closes below the HMA
- The RSI crosses below 50

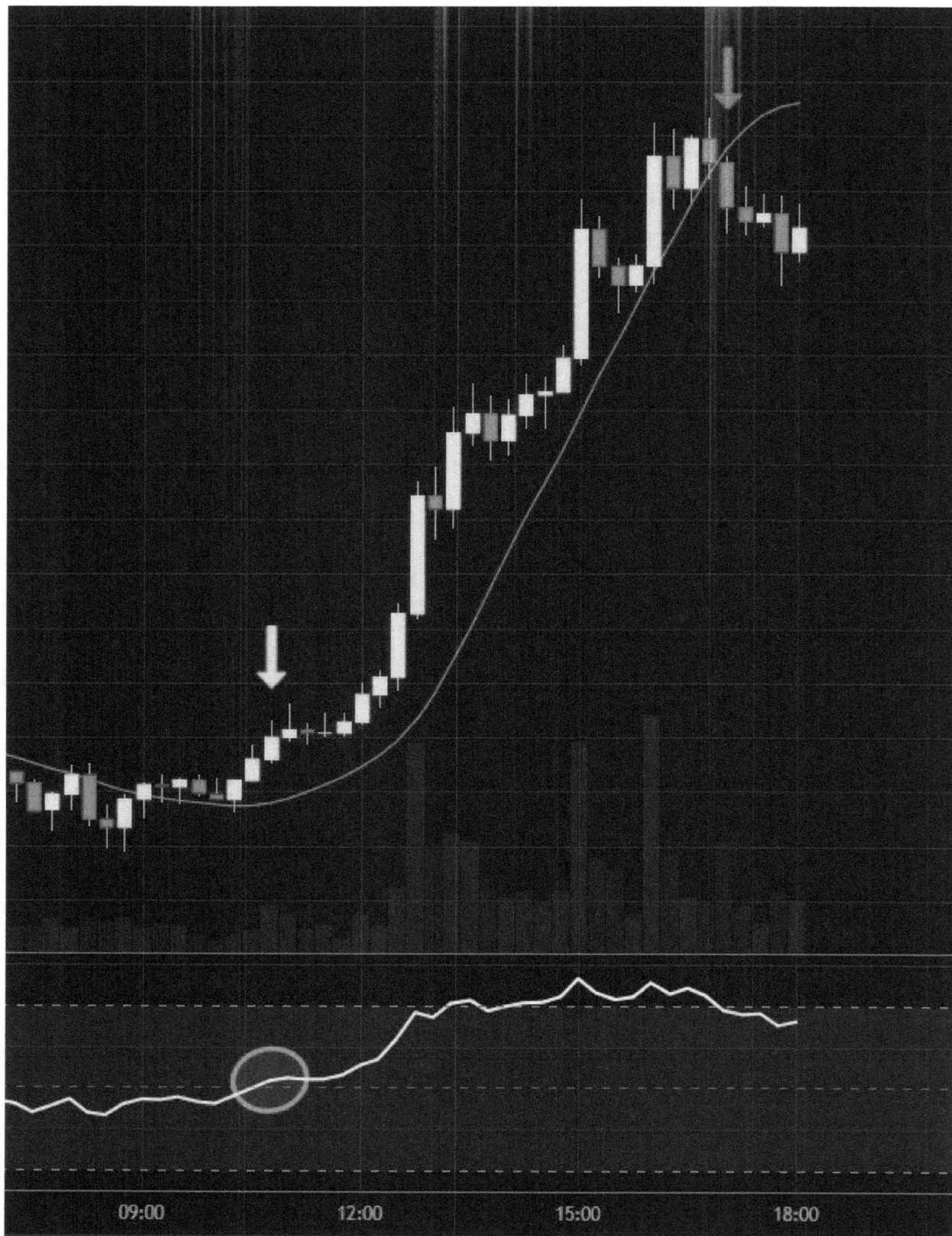

An example of a entry (green arrow) and exit (red arrow) using this strategy

Strategy #8: DiDi Indicator + QQE

Strategy Overview: This strategy uses the DiDi indicator and the QQE indicator to enter emerging trends and exit them before they reverse.

Step 1) Add the Indicators
For this strategy we will add three indicators on our chart:

- 12 SMA

- Quantitative Qualitative Estimation indicator QQE –TradingView community indicator by KivancOzbilgic

- Didi Index Improved with QQE | jh - TradingView community indicator by jiehonglim

Step 2) BuyConditions
Enter the trade only when all of these rules are met:

- Candles are closing above the 12 SMA

- The DiDi histogram (dots) are green

- Buy when the QQE crosses up and shows a buy signal

Step 3) Sell Conditions

Close the trade or take profits if one of these conditions occurs:

- A candle closes below the 12 SMA

- The QQE crosses down and shows a sell signal

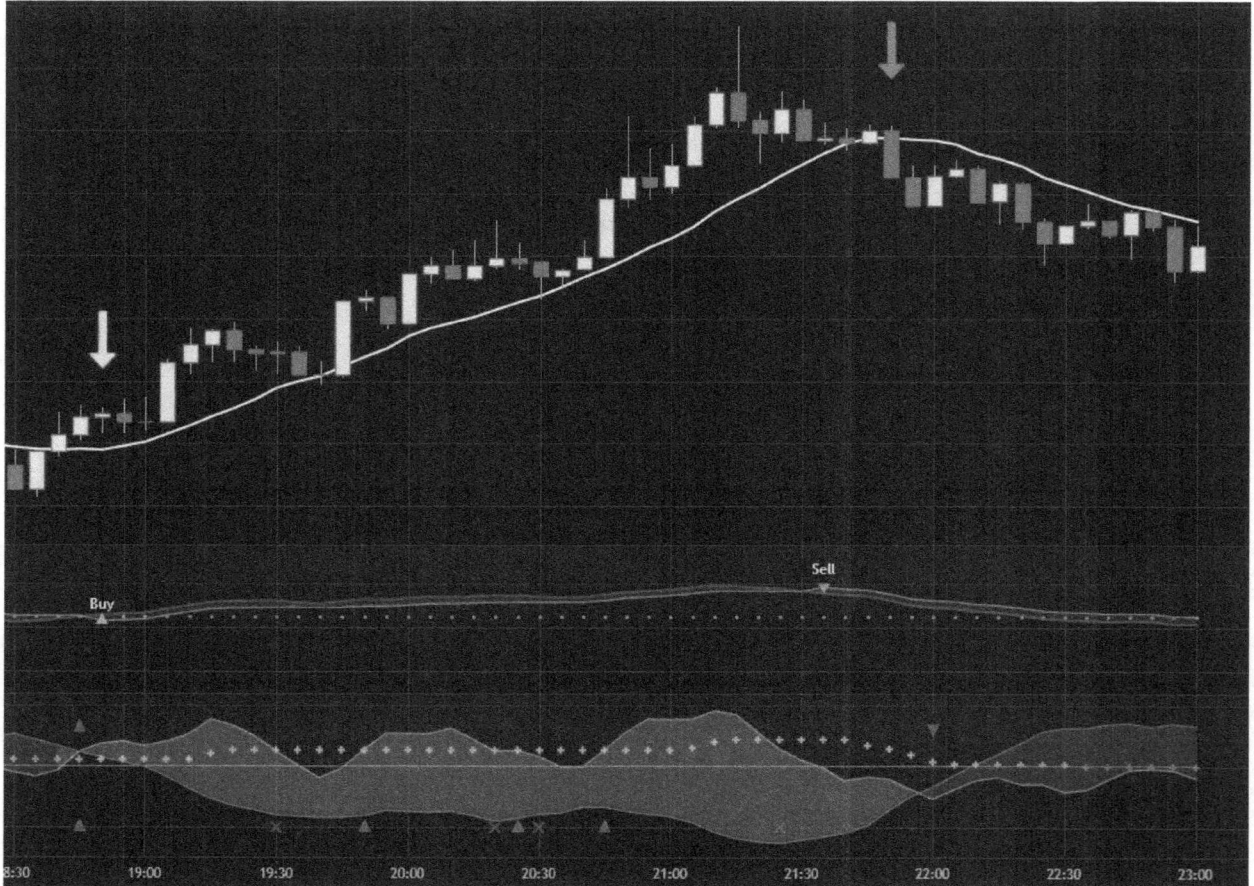

Example of a long entry (green arrow) and exit (red arrow) using this strategy

Strategy #9: Scalp Pro Indicator Scalping Strategy

Strategy Overview:

This is a scalping strategy that works best on the 5 minute timeframe and lower. When using this strategy trade in the same trend direction as the daily timeframe.

Step 1) Add the Indicators

For this strategy we will add three indicators on our chart:

- 200 MA

- 20 HMA (Hull moving average)

- Scalp pro - Change the smooth length to 10

The Scalp pro is a community indicator on TradingView, to find it type "scalp pro" in the indicator search box, author is ovelix.

Step 2) Buy Conditions

Enter the trade only when all of these rules are met:

- Price is above the 200 MA

- A candle closes above the HMA

- The Scalp pro crosses up and a buy signal appears

Step 3) Sell Conditions

Close the trade or take profits if one of these conditions occurs.

- A candle closes below the HMA
- The Scalp Pro crosses down and a sell signal appears

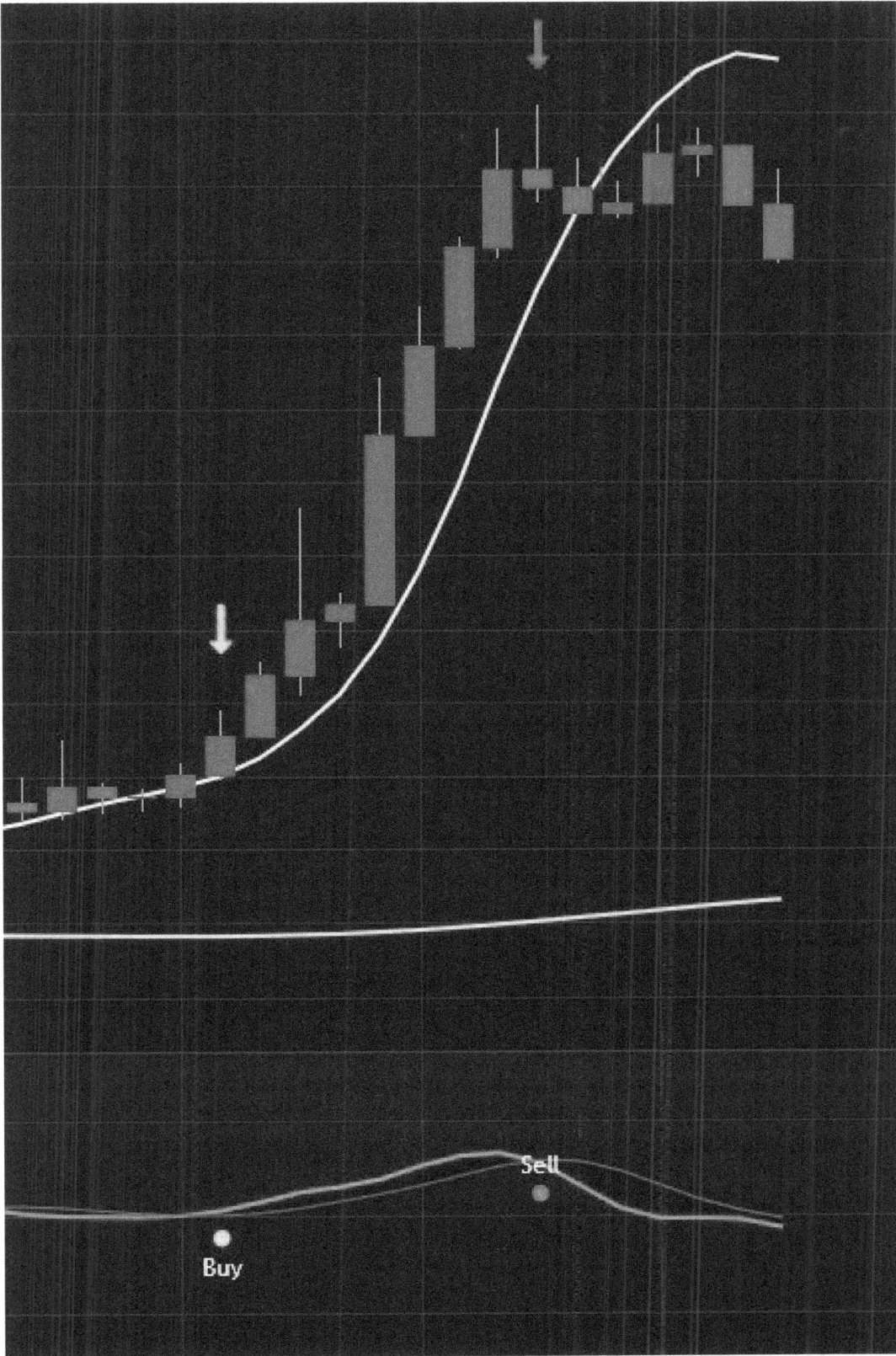

Example of a entry (green arrow) and exit (red arrow) using this strategy

Strategy #10: Bjorgum SuperScript+ QQE

Required Indicators:

- Bjorgum SuperScript (TradingView community indicator)
- Quantitative Qualitative Estimation QQE (TradingView community indicator)
- 200 SMA

Buy Conditions:

- Price is above the 200 SMA
- A candle turns yellow or blue and closes above the BJSuperScript indicator
- Enter when the QQE crosses up and displays a buy signal

Sell Conditions:

- The BJSuperScript turns red

Or

- The QQE crosses down and a sell signal appears

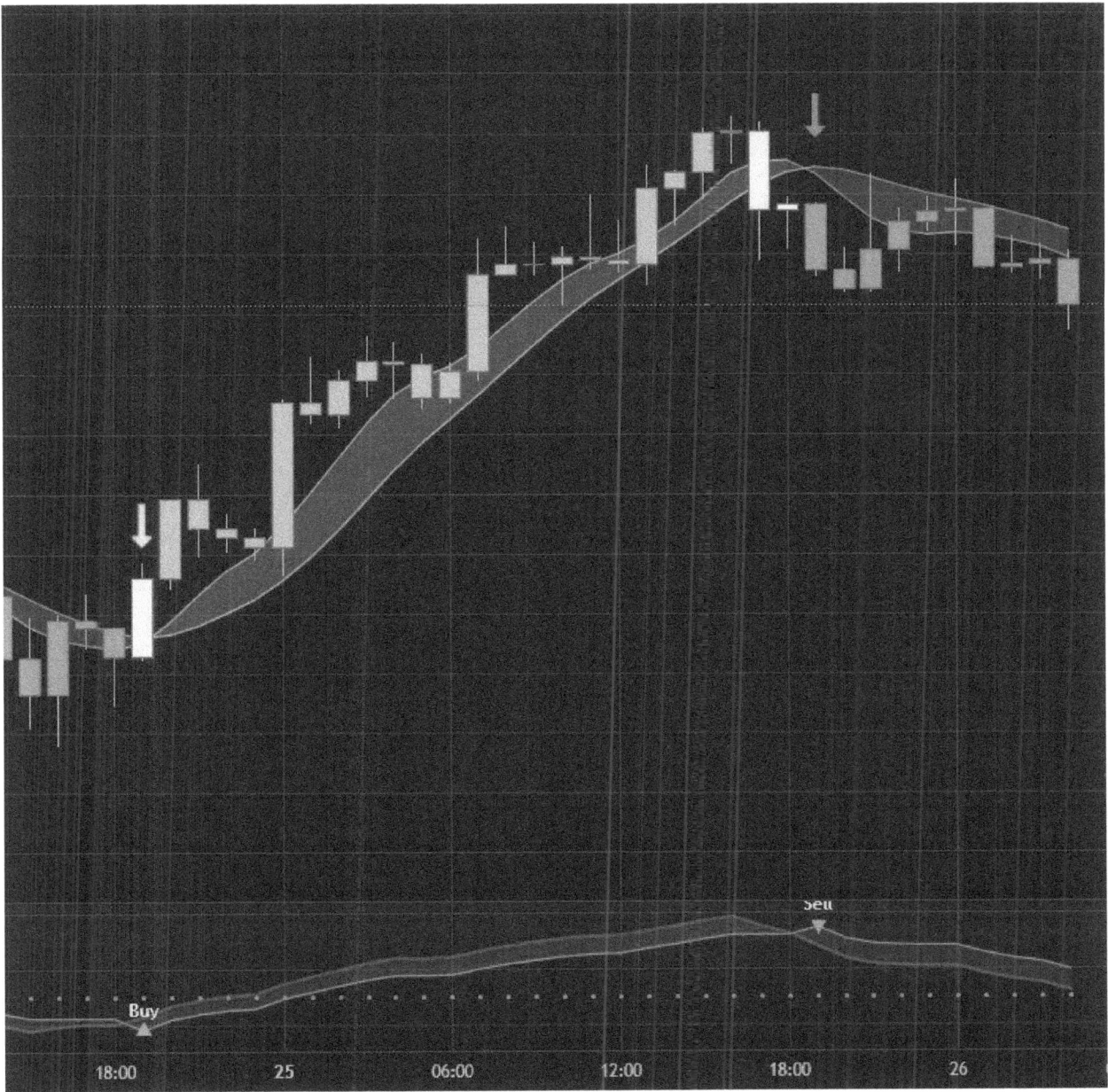

Example of a buy (green arrow) and sell (red arrow) using this strategy

Strategy #11: Aroon Scalping Strategy

Strategy Overview:

This is a day trading strategy but it can also be used as a swing trading strategy on the higher timeframes. His strategy uses the Aroon indicator for entries and exits.

Step 1) Add the Indicators

For this strategy we will add three indicators on our chart:

- Aroon indicator

- 14 period RSI

- 10 SMA (simple moving average

Step 2) Buy Conditions

Enter the trade only when all of these rules are met.

- The RSI crosses above 50

- Price is above the 10 SMA

- Buy when the aroon up line crosses above the aroon down line

Step 3) Sell Conditions

Close the trade or take profits if one of these conditions occurs:

- A candle closes below the 10 SMA

- The aroon up crosses below 80

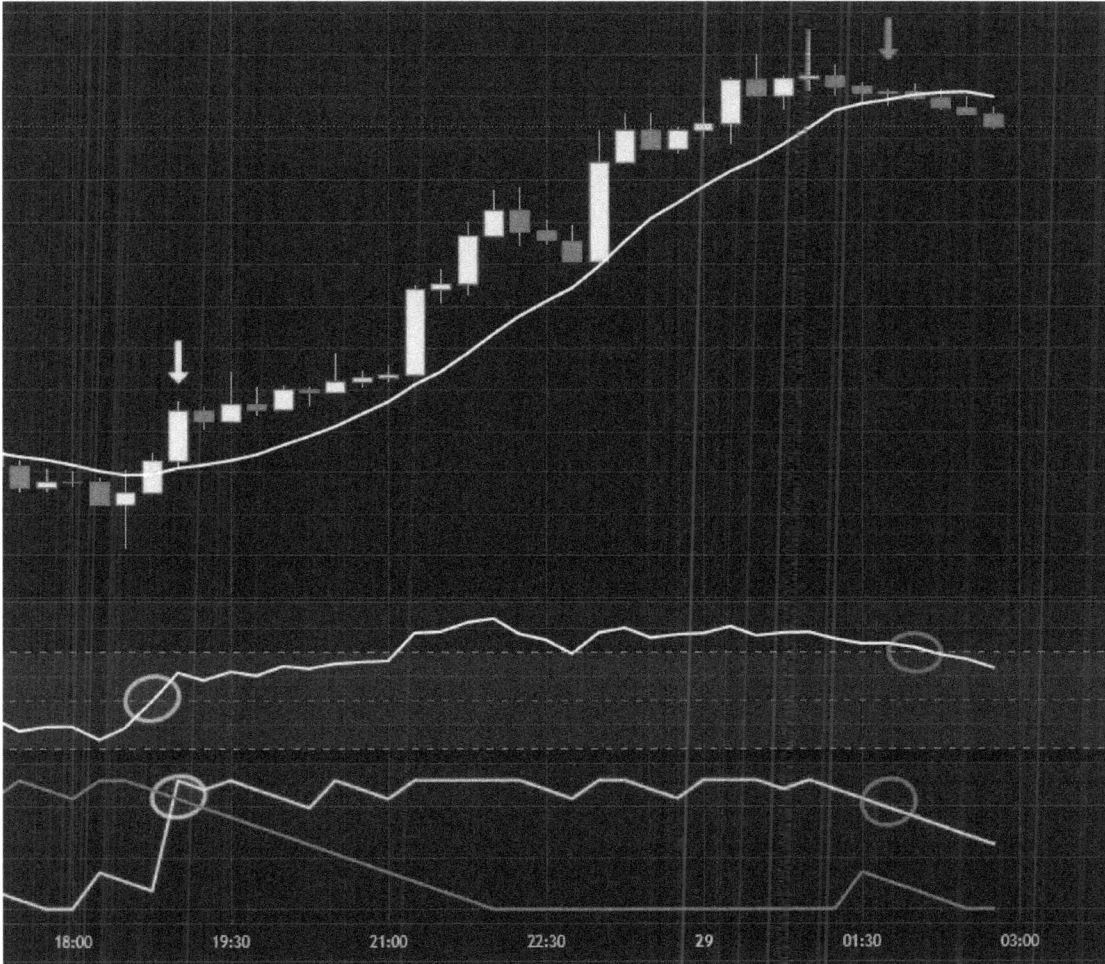

Example of a long entry (green arrow) and exit (red arrow) using this strategy

Strategy #12: Bollinger Band and RSI Scalping Strategy

Strategy Overview:

This is a scalping strategy using the Bollinger bands and RSI indicators. To get the best results when using this strategy trade in the direction of the daily trend.

Step 1) Add the Indicators

For this strategy we will add three indicators on our chart:

- 15 period HMA (Hull moving average)
- 5 period RSI
- Bollinger bands with settings

Length = 20, Stdev = 2.5

Step 2) Buy Conditions

Enter the trade only when all of these rules are met.

- The RSI is oversold
- A candle is below or touching the bottom Bollinger band
- Buy when a candle closes above the HMA

Step 3) Sell Conditions

Close the trade or take profits if one of these conditions occurs:

- The RSI is overbought

- A candle closes below the HMA

Example of a entry (green arrow) and exit (red arrow) using this strategy

Strategy #13: RSI + VWMA Scalping Strategy

Strategy Overview:

This strategy uses a RSI with a VWMA (volume weighted moving average) on the RSI. Entry and exit signals occur when the RSI and moving average crossover. This strategy can be used for both scalping and day trading.

Step 1) Add the Indicators

For this strategy we will add three indicators on our chart:

- 10 MA

- 200 MA

- 14 period RSI

- 20 period VWMA added on the RSI

Step 2) Buy Conditions

Enter the trade only when all of these rules are met:

- Candles are closing above the 200 MA

- The RSI crosses above the VWMA

- Candles are closing above the 10 MA

Step 3) Sell Conditions

Close the trade or take profits if one of these conditions occurs:

- A candle closes below the 10 MA

- The RSI crosses below the VWMA

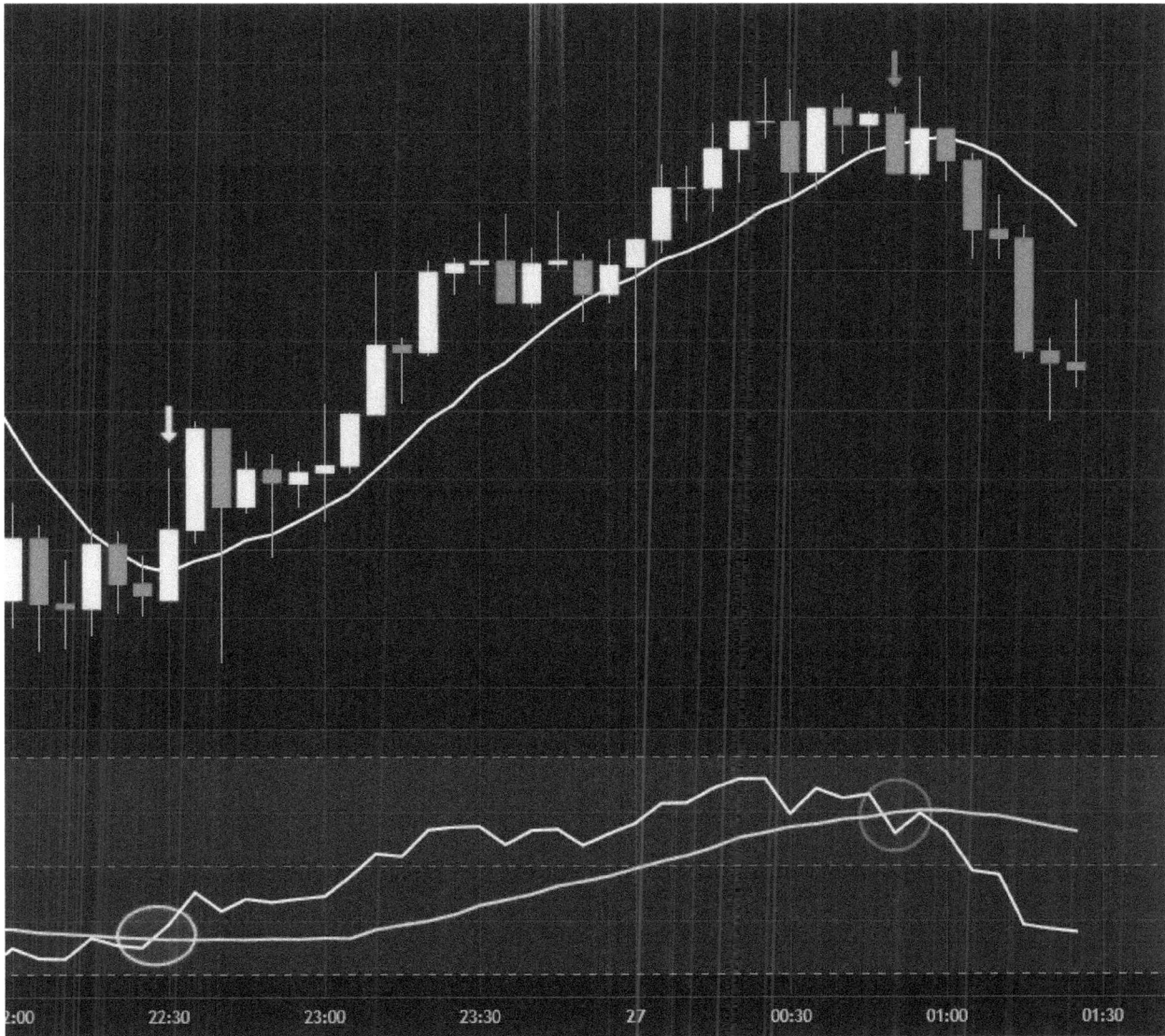

Example of a entry (green arrow) and exit (red arrow) using this strategy

Strategy #14: Easy RSI Scalping Strategy

Strategy Overview:
This is a quick scalping strategy that works best on the lower time frame charts (5 min and lower). When using this strategy, only take trades that are in the direction of the daily trend.

Step 1) Add the Indicators
For this strategy we will add three indicators on our chart:

- 100 period HMA (Hull moving average)
- 5 period RSI

Step 2) Buy Conditions
Enter the trade only when all of these rules are met.

- The RSI is above 50
- Buy when a candle closes above the 100 HMA

Step 3) Sell Conditions
Close the trade or take profits if one of these conditions occurs:

- The RSI crosses above 85, or the RSI below 70 after being overbought
- A candle closes below the HMA

Example of an entry (green arrow) and exit (red arrow) using this strategy

Strategy #15: Awesome Oscillator Strategy

Strategy Overview:

This is a day trading strategy that uses the awesome oscillator to enter emerging trends early, and exit them when they reverse.

Step 1) Add the Indicators

For this strategy we will add three indicators on our chart:

- 10 period SMMA (smooth moving average)

- AO (Awesome oscillator)

- RSI, length set to 7

Step 2) Buy Conditions

Enter the trade only when all of these rules are met:

- The RSI is above 50

- The AO is green

- Candles are closing above the SMMA

Step 3) Sell Conditions

Close the trade or take profits if one of these conditions occurs:

- A candle closes below the SMMA

- The RSI crosses below 50 and the AO is red

Example of a entry (green circle) using this strategy

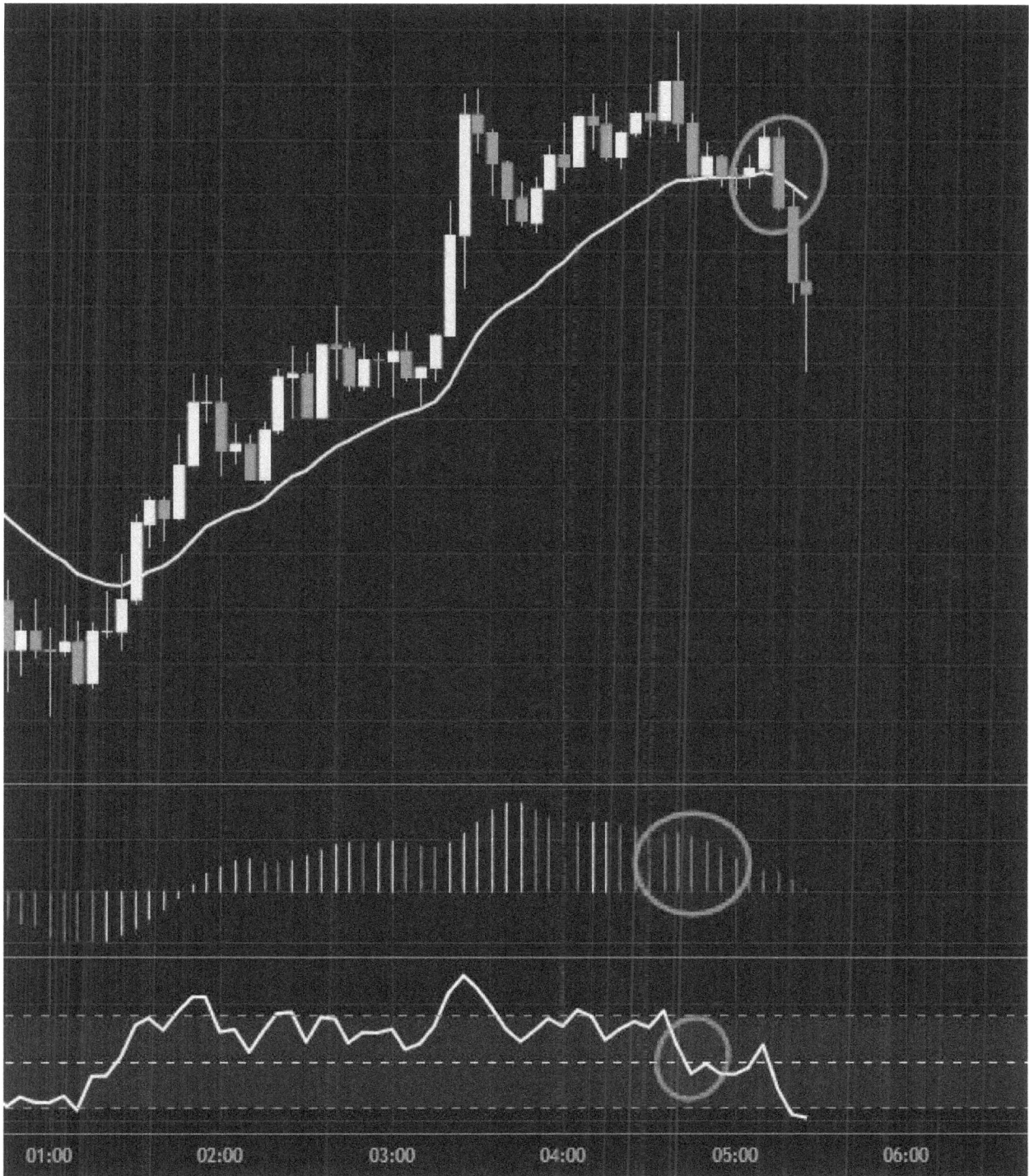

Example of a exit (red circle) using this strategy

Strategy #16: Moving Average Crossover Strategy

Strategy Overview: This is a moving average crossover strategy that uses a combination of three moving averages – one HMA and two SMMAs. Entry signals will occur when the SMMA cross, and the HMA will be used for exiting the trade.

Step 1) Add the Indicators
For this strategy we will add three indicators on our chart:

- 8 SMMA (smoothed moving average
- 3 SMMA
- 34 HMA (hull moving average)

Step 2) Buy Conditions
Enter the trade only when all of these rules are met:

- Candles are closing above the 34 HMA
- Buy when the 3 SMMA crosses over the 8 SMMA
- Place a stop loss under the low of the entry candle

Step 3) Sell Conditions
Close the trade or take profits if one of these conditions occurs:

- A candle closes below the 34 HMA

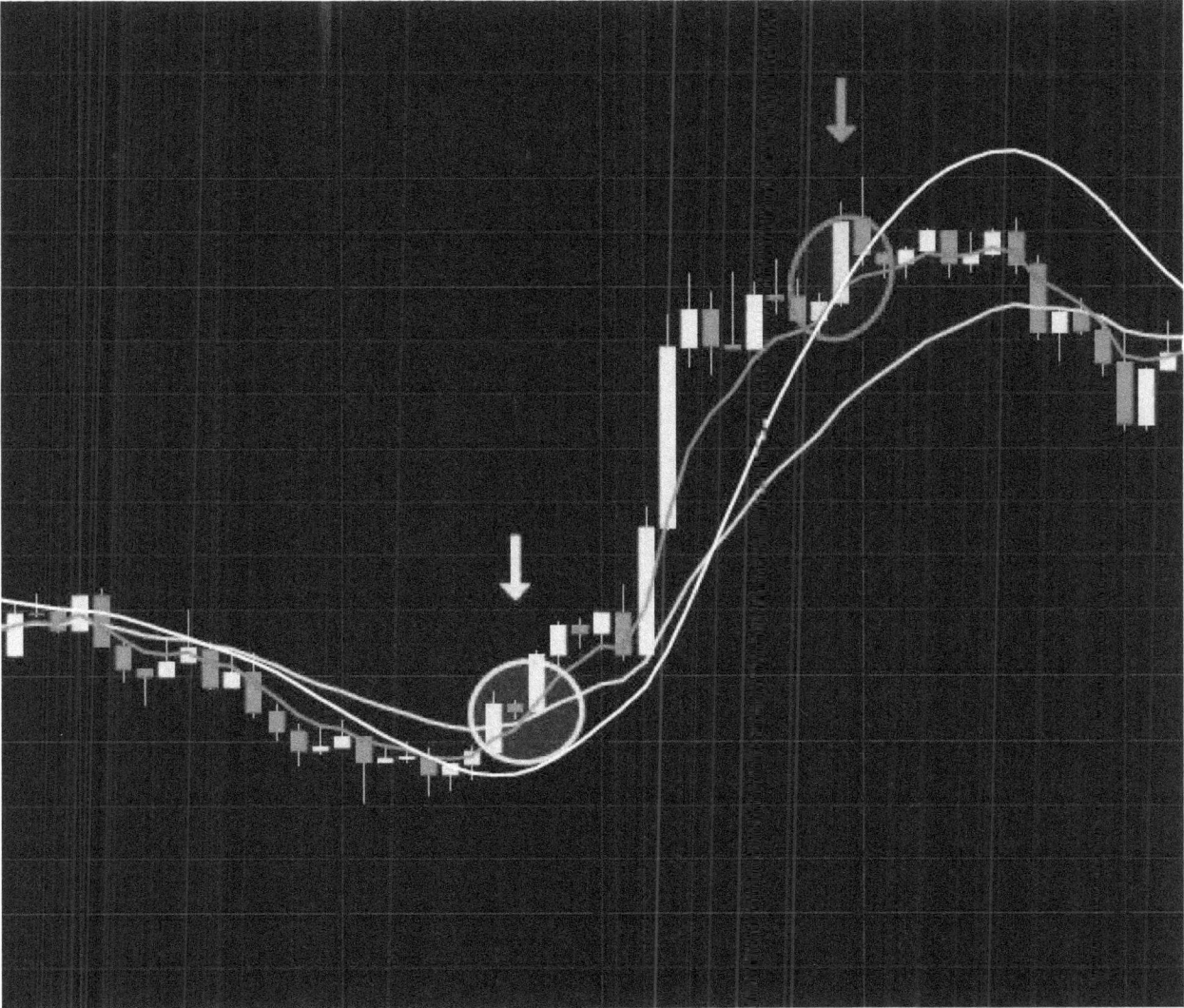

Example of a buy (green circle) and exit (red circle) signal using this strategy

Strategy #17: 1000 SMA Scalping Strategy

Strategy Overview: This strategy uses the 1000 SMA for trading bounces off it. This is a scalping strategy that will work best on the 1 minute timeframe chart.

Step 1) Add the Indicators

For this strategy we will add three indicators on our chart:

- 200 EMA

- 1000 sma (simple moving average)

- Stochastic with settings:

K = 14, D = 3, Smooth K = 6

Step 2) Buy Conditions

Enter the trade only when all of these rules are met:

- The 200 EMA is above the 1000 SMA

- Price drops below the 200 EMA

- The stochastics are below 20

- Buy when a candle touches the 1000 SMA, place a stop loss under the low of the entry candle

Step 3) Sell Conditions

Close the trade or take profits if one of these conditions occurs:

- Price touches the 200 EMA

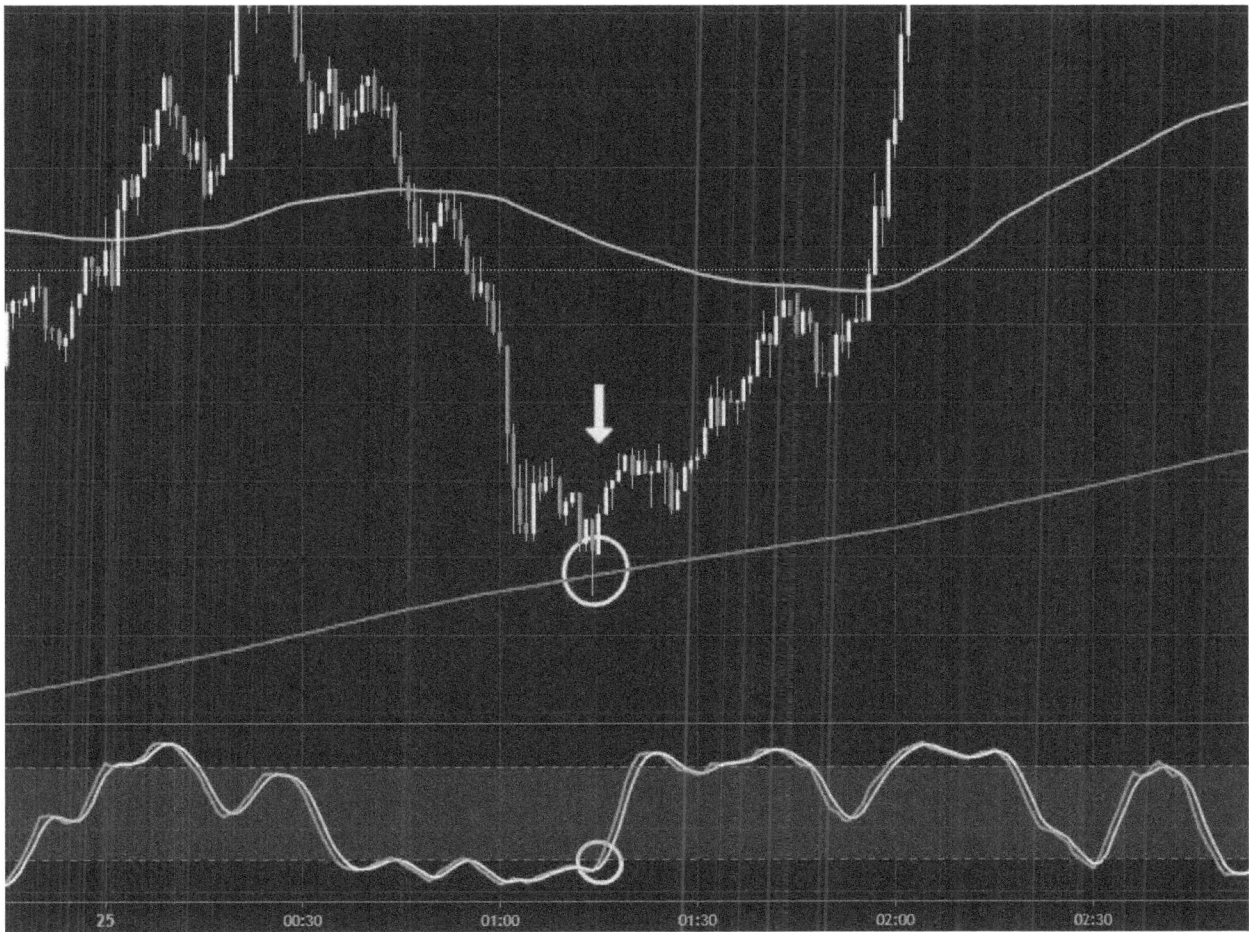

Example of a buy signal using this strategy

Strategy #18: WMA Momentum Strategy

Strategy Overview: This is a momentum trading strategy using the weighted moving average and RSI. The RSI is used to indicate increasing momentum and the weighted moving average will be used to confirm the trend.

Step 1) Add the Indicators

For this strategy we will add three indicators on our chart:

- 20 WMA (weighted moving average)
- RSI, Length = 7

Step 2) Buy Conditions

Enter the trade only when all of these rules are met:

- A candle closes above the 20 WMA
- The RSI is above 50

Step 3) Sell Conditions

Close the trade or take profits if one of these conditions occurs:

Example of a entry (green circle) using this strategy

Example of a exit (red circle) using this strategy

www.ingramcontent.com/pod-product-compliance
Lightning Source LLC
Chambersburg PA
CBHW081745200326
41597CB00024B/4397